UNESCO/FOREST

ANTHOLOGY OF CHUV

GENNADY AYGI was born in 19: Shaymurzino, in the southern part of the Chuvash Republic, some 500 miles east of Moscow. His father was a teacher of Russian; his mother's father was one of the last pagan priests. He studied at the Gorky Literary Institute in Moscow, and during these years became friendly with Boris Pasternak, who encouraged him to go over to writing poetry in Russian. For several years he was employed at the Mayakovsky Museum in Moscow, where he became an expert on the modernist art and literature of the early twentieth century and was one of the 'underground' generation of writers and artists.

After being dismissed from his post in 1969, he led a life of creative hardship, attracting considerable hostility, receiving almost no official recognition, and earning his living principally as a translator into Chuvash. He has translated poems from several languages, including Russian, French, Polish and Hungarian, into his native tongue; his highly successful anthology of French poetry, published in 1968, was awarded a prize by the Académie Française.

His own poetry, written in Russian, is among the most original work of our time; it is grouped into numerous books, but almost none of it had been published in the Soviet Union before 1987. It has however been published abroad, both in the original and in translation into almost all the languages of Europe (an English translation of *Veronica's Book* by Peter France was published by Polygon Books in 1989). He is now widely regarded as one of the most important poets writing in Russian, and is at last being recognized in the Soviet Union. He lives with his wife in Moscow, and has six children.

PETER FRANCE was born in Londonderry in 1935. He went to school in Yorkshire and studied French and Russian at Oxford and in France. From 1963 to 1980 he worked at the University of Sussex; since then he has been Professor of French at Edinburgh University. As well as writing extensively about French literature, he is the author of *Poets of Modern Russia* (Cambridge, 1982), and has published translations of works by Rousseau, Diderot, Blok (with Jon Stallworthy), Pasternak (with Jon Stallworthy), and the contemporary poets Gennady Aygi, Joseph Brodsky and Oleg Chukhontsev. He visited Chuvashia in 1989 and is currently working with Gennady Aygi on an anthology of Scottish poetry in Chuvash.

A N

CHUVASH
ANTHOLOGY OF
POETRY

An Anthology
Compiled and
Introduced by
Gennady Aygi

Translated by
Peter France

FOREST
BOOKS
London & Boston

UNESCO

UNESCO COLLECTION OF REPRESENTATIVE WORKS
NON-RUSSIAN LANGUAGES OF THE USSR SERIES

PUBLISHED BY
FOREST BOOKS
20 Forest View, London E4 7AY, U.K.
61 Lincoln Road, Wayland, MA 01778, U.S.A.

FIRST PUBLISHED 1991

Typeset in Great Britain by Cover to Cover, Cambridge
Printed in Great Britain by BPCC Wheatons Ltd., Exeter

The copyright in the original Chuvash poems is retained by the
different authors or their heirs who approved the publication
of the present translation
English translations © Peter France 1991
Introduction and Epilogue © UNESCO 1991

ALL RIGHTS RESERVED

British Library Cataloguing in Publication Data
An Anthology of Chuvash Poetry
1. Turkic poetry
I. France, Peter 1935— II. UNESCO
894.3

Library of Congress Catalogue Card No:
90–86404

ISBN 1 85610 003 0

Contents

II. Songs and Speeches

III. Poems and ethnographic writing
of the modern period

Chavash Khveti

Translator's Preface

This anthology has been compiled by one of the most significant poets writing in Russian today, Gennady Aygi. Aygi is also a Chuvash writer. He was born in 1934 in Shaymurzino, a village in the Chuvash Autonomous Republic of the U.S.S.R., and although since about 1960 he has written most of his own poetry in Russian, he has continued to write in his native tongue. Most importantly, he has translated volumes of poetry into Chuvash from a number of European languages (French, Polish and Hungarian), thus contributing notably to making modern Western culture accessible in this small country on the eastern margin of Europe.

The present volume is an attempt to make the English-speaking world aware of the Chuvash, to allow the voice of Aygi's people to be heard across the world. In translating it, I came to feel a great affection for this people, and this was much enhanced when in September 1989 I was able to visit Chuvashia as a guest of the Chuvash Writers' Union, and to enjoy the hospitality which figures so prominently in this anthology. I do not, however, know more than a few words of the Chuvash language. This translation has been done from Russian versions prepared by Aygi, who is equally at home in both languages. Though I have heard many of the Chuvash originals read aloud, and have made some use of Aygi's indications concerning rhyme and metre, I have not tried to imitate the prosody or sonority of the Chuvash texts in any detail. As far as the sense goes, I am most grateful to Professor John R. Krueger of Indiana University, who has ready many of the Chuvash poems and feels that in general my translations adequately reflect the content of the originals.

In transliterating Russian and Chuvash names, I have generally followed the system used in Britain in books designed for a non-specialist public; I have not transcribed the Russian soft sign or any Chuvash diacritics. At the head of the poems by each author (and in the table of contents) the names are given in their Chuvash version; the Russian version is given underneath, and this is the one used in the

Introduction and Epilogue. In most cases the voiced consonants of the Russian version correspond more accurately to the actual pronunciation. In the texts themselves I have retained a certain number of Chuvash words which designate specifically Chuvash items of clothing, rituals, etc.; these are glossed in brief footnotes.

This publication is meant for a general reading public. Those who are interested in further reading can consult the following English language publications, which also contain further bibliographical indications: J.R. Krueger, *Chuvash Manual* (Indiana University Publications, Uralic and Altaic series, No. 7), Indiana University Press and Mouton, The Hague, 1961; Laszlo Vikár and Gabor Bereczki, *Chuvash Folksongs*, Akadémiai Kiadó, Budapest, 1979; A. Róna-Tas, *Chuvash Studies*, Akadémiai Kiadó, Budapest, 1983.

It remains only for me to offer my thanks to all those who have helped me in my work on this anthology: to Porphiry Afanasyev, President of the Chuvash Writers' Union, to Atner Khuzangay and all my other Chuvash friends too numerous to mention here, to John H. Krueger and Léon Robel, to M. Edouard J. Maunick and Mlle Francoise Laporte of UNESCO, and above all, of course, to my dear friend Gennady Aygi.

Peter France
Edinburgh, 1991

Introduction

To the memory of my mother Khevedus, daughter of Yagur,
of the family of Yumankka

I

Who are the Chuvash? Where is their home? What can be said in a few words about their history, their language, their beliefs, their culture?

For the most part they live on the right bank of the Volga, between the Gorky region and Kazan, in the territory of the Chuvash Autonomous Socialist Republic. In the 1979 census, the population of the Republic was given as 1,292,000, of whom 68.4% were Chuvash, the rest being made up of Russians, Tatars and Mari. The Chuvash language is also spoken outside the Republic, principally in the Bashkir and Tatar Autonomous Republics and in the Ulyanov, Kuybyshev, Orenburg, Saratov and Penza regions of the RSFSR. According to the 1979 census, there are 1,751,000 Chuvash in the whole of the Soviet Union.

'There is hardly another people in the Soviet Union whose origins have attracted as much attention . . . as the Chuvash', said the Russian linguist B. Serebrennikov in 1956. 'There are good reasons for this intense interest, the main one being the Chuvash language, which is so original and so different from the other related Turkic languages that the scholar is forced to consider the cause of this originality, and to ask whether it is not bound up with some mysterious historical roots of the Chuvash people.' And indeed the Chuvash have been identified with all manner of peoples: the Khazars, the Sumerians, the Basques, the Sarmatians and the less familiar Avars and Burtasses.

The generally accepted conclusions about the genesis of this people may be summarized as follows. The most ancient known forebears of the Turkic-speaking peoples are the Hunnish tribes known as the Bulgars and the Suvars. In the second century B.C., they were driven westwards by the Chinese and settled in central Asia; in the following century, they crossed the Volga and occupied the steppes between the Caspian Sea and the Sea of Azov. Subsequently, the main body of the Huns moved as far west as the Danube.

After the death of Attila in 453 A.D., the power of the Huns collapsed. (As late as the nineteenth century the name 'Adila' was common among the Chuvash, and even today the Volga is called 'Atal'.) Then, in the seventh century, the kingdom of Greater Bulgaria, which had grown up on the steppes by the Sea of Azov and in Transcaucasia, gave way to the onslaught of the Khazars. A number of Bulgarian tribes (the so-called 'black Bulgars') moved west and in 681 settled in the territory of present-day Bulgaria. They mingled with the local Slavonic population, adopted their language, but kept their own customs and beliefs until the conversion to Christianity of their king Boris at the beginning of the ninth century. Various Chuvash words survived in the language of the Bulgarians, and to this day there are similarities in the customs and rituals, the women's costume, the headgear and ornaments of the Bulgarians and the Chuvash.

(The idea of this anthology came to me fifteen years ago from a kind of vision or waking dream I once had. I was sitting on the steps in front of a wooden house in Cheboksary, the Chuvash capital, reading the typescript of my Chuvash anthology of French poetry. Perhaps out of longing for something ancient in our native writing, I suddenly thought of the Old Bulgarian monuments, of which I only knew a few 'non-poetic' epitaphs. It was a windy spring day. Far off on the Tatar steppes, among the grasses, stood those lonely rectangular burial columns with inscriptions in Arabic writing. They were also standing, orphan-like, on the steppes of the Ulyanov region and the fields of South-East Chuvashia. I dreamed of mysterious lines of 'funeral poetry' – stone words on stone . . . And the first texts I looked at for my Chuvash anthology were to be these epitaphs of the thirteenth and fourteenth centuries. There were indeed lines of verse on them, but only Arabic sayings from the Koran. Nevertheless, these inscriptions are the first monuments of Chuvash writing; the non-Arabic words on them – dates, proper names, circumstances of death – are the same as Chuvash words . . . The spring wind of the 1960s was blowing the steppe grass against the names of the Bulgars on these tombs, and it was the ancestors of these Bulgars, thirteen centuries ago, who had travelled to the distant Danube.)

The second group of Bulgarian-Suvarian tribes, the 'silver Bulgars', settled on the central Volga, while the third made its way to the foothills of the Caucasus. In the tenth century, the Bulgars and Suvars who were dependent on the Khazar khanate (and therefore temporarily influenced by Judaism, the official religion of the Khazars) united into a single state, known as Eastern Bulgaria. This was the first state on the central Volga, and came into being at more or less the same time as Ancient Russia (*Rus*). After the defeat of the Khazars by Ancient Russia (actively supported by the Bulgars), the Bulgar kingdom on the Volga developed rapidly. In the second half of the tenth century, cities grew up along the Volga: Bolgar (the capital), Suvar, Bilyar, Oshel and others. The Bulgar kings had sizeable armies and minted their own coinage. There was an active trade between the Bulgars and both the Russians and countries to the east. The old Russian chronicles mention military expeditions against Eastern Bulgaria as well as Bulgar raids on Russian territory. After the founding of Nizhny-Novgorod in 1221, the Russians gradually expanded on to neighbouring territories and found themselves living alongside the Hunnish-Bulgarian ancestors of the Chuvash.

It is generally held today that the Chuvash people was finally formed between the thirteenth and fifteenth centuries from a mingling of the related Bulgars and Suvars, with an admixture of the original Finno-Ugrian population of the area. As for the language, with its two dialects ('Upper' and 'Lower'), research has shown that it developed from Old Bulgarian, which like the other Turkic languages belongs to the Uralo-Altaic family. It contains many borrowings from other Turkic languages, as well as from the Arabic, Iranian, Mongolian and Finno-Ugrian languages, from Old Hebrew and from Byzantine Greek. It is particularly noteworthy that there are several hundred words related to the Mongolian, which are absent from the other Turkic languages or have a somewhat different meaning in them. They are words of ancient origin, dating from the time when the Chuvash were neighbours of the Mongol tribes of Central Asia; this appears to show that the ancestor of the Chuvash language occupied an intermediate position between the Turkic and the Mongolian.

II

For several centuries the Bulgars used the runic writing they had brought from the south. Then, in the tenth century, Islam was established in Eastern Bulgaria and Arabic writing gradually replaced runes. At the same time, hieroglyphs and Chinese characters were also in use. The names of several learned men of this period have survived, including the twelfth-century historian Nadim, author of a history of Bulgaria. Relics of the ancient Chuvash writing have reached us in embroidery, tribal signs and craftsmen's marks.

Although the Bulgar feudal overlords had adopted Islam, the majority of the Bulgars from the tenth to the thirteenth century remained pagans. The year 1229 saw the first Christian martyr, a merchant from Bolgar who was put to death for trying to further the spread of his religion; he was canonized under the name of Avraamy the Bulgar, and is still revered by the Russian Orthodox Church.

In 1236, an immense Mongol Tatar army, having crushed the stubborn resistance of the Bulgars, seized the territory of Eastern Bulgaria. The domination of the Golden Horde, which lasted over 200 years, led to such a decline in the culture of the Chuvash that they lost their writing. They flocked into the dense forests beyond the Kama river and on the right bank of the Volga, where they could not be reached by the conquerors. A part of the Bulgarian population were converted to Islam and became Tatars. The others, whose nucleus was the Suvars and the Chuvash, defended their language, their customs and their religion even under the domination of the Khanate of Kazan, which began in the early fifteenth century.

The ancient pagan religion of the Chuvash has still not been adequately studied, and the complete Pantheon of Chuvash deities has yet to be reconstructed. Of the numerous pagan prayers, spells and charms which have been collected in the last seventy years, only a handful have been published in Chuvashia. For this reason, in the present anthology I have used mainly anthologies produced in Hungary and Finland.

The supreme god of the Chuvash Pantheon was *Tura*, who is usually connected with the Altaic *Tengri* (sky god). Taking no direct part in human affairs, he controlled them through the gods *Kebe*, who knew all the destinies of the human race, *Piulekh*, who allotted good or bad fortune, and *Pigambar*, who distributed spiritual qualities and sent prophetic visions to the priests and magicians – Pigambar also had a Promethean function as the 'giver of fire to all the universe'.

The Earth was an object of particular veneration to the Chuvash, who deified her under the name of *Ama* (Mother). She was surrounded by a whole family of spirits of the Earth (see 'Prayer at the Festival of the Sacrificial Beer Offering'). There is an extraordinary wealth of forms and images arising from the Chuvash deification of the Earth, the Sun, the Air, Fire and Water. Then among the minor deities there were the creators and protectors of people, crops, cattle, bees and so forth.

Like other religions, that of the Chuvash was characterized by dualism. Opposed to the good deities was a special group of evil deities, chief among whom was *Shuittan*. The most noteworthy of these are *Esrel* (god of death), *Ierekh* (sender of external ailments), *Iye* (the house spirit) and *Arzyuri* (the wood spirit).

The religious life of the Chuvash centred not on particular individuals (the shamanistic elect who can see spirits), but on collective sacrificial offerings to the various classes of gods and spirits. In particular it centred on the *kiremet*, a term of Arabic derivation which in Chuvash mythology designates a category of spirits who are the souls of exceptional ancestors and magicians of former times. The name was also given to the sanctuaries used for the worship of these spirits. Almost every Chuvash village had its *kiremet*.

The sacrifices and other rituals were conducted by elders and especially venerable people, who were also priests in the ordinary sense of the word (as opposed to the *yumozi* or magicians). In fact, the Chuvash language has no fixed word for priest; in different places he might be given different names: Keeper of the Sacrifice, Leader of the Prayers, Leader of the Sacrificial Offering, Overseer of the *Kiremet* (my maternal grandfather was the last Overseer of the *Kiremet* in our village). The priests were appointed by the village community on the basis of general trust in their deep knowledge of the meaning and details of the rituals, their wisdom and their moral qualities. They remained ordinary peasants in their daily life, while retaining their authority in all areas of communal life.

The most important collective rituals, all connected with the agricultural cycle, were the *Ui Chyuge* (Field Sacrifice), the *Syumor Chyuge* (Rain Prayers) and the *Sora Chyuge* (Thanksgiving Offering of Beer, and prayer to all the deities who govern the world of men). Prayers and sacrifices were also offered in every family, with the head of the house officiating. And apart from the sacrifices, there were several other religious festivals: *Surkhuri* (the winter festival of young people, with prayers for a good harvest and an increase of cattle), *Kalom* (a spring festival of several days' duration in honour of Tura and a communal commemoration of the dead – on the last days of this festival was celebrated the *Seren*, a ritual exorcizing evil spirits), *Simek* (The festival of spring flowering, with memorial prayers in the cemeteries), *Sinze* (the Pregnancy of the Earth, when it was forbidden to disturb the Earth, to tread on Her with bare feet, to work in the fields or to take stones from Her), *Yuba* (collective memorial prayers in autumn).

Alongside the cult of spirits, the cult of ancestors had an immense importance in Chuvash religious life. This anthology includes the poetic text 'Festivals' by N. Okhotnikov, which shows what deep feelings of the inseparability of the dead and the living were called forth by the memorial prayers for the dead. In all the Chuvash religious rituals one can sense the powerful yet unobtrusive presence of the 'archetypal' layers of the consciousness of the ancient Chuvash, close to the 'secrets of nature' (to quote Jacob Boehme) – see for instance in this anthology the moving account by V. Magnitsky of the 'stealing of the earth'.

Before ending this brief account of the ancient religion of the Chuvash, let me mention just one more archaic ritual, *Kher agi*, which suggests the pristine closeness of man to the earth. It means 'maidens' ploughing'. Grown-up girls would harness themselves to the plough with unbelted dresses and loose hair; then, in the dead calm of night, when everything human was silent, they would plough a furrow round the village, at a distance of one or two miles. During this time, no-one was allowed on the roads, whether from the village or outside it, and anyone who tried to approach the place of ploughing was beaten with rowan twigs (the rowan had magic powers). When the ploughing was over, fire was kindled by rubbing pieces of oak wood together, eggs were fried, and the fire was carried into the village houses. This ritual disappeared in the 1880s. Scholars can only speculate about its meaning; was it the tracing of a magic circle for protection against epidemics, or perhaps also a symbolic return to matriarchal times, when the earth was ploughed by women?

III

The Khanate of Kazan, whose rulers in the sixteenth century became vassals of the Sultan of Turkey, was a serious threat to the Russian state. For over 100 years Russia and Kazan were in conflict, largely on Chuvash soil. The year 1469 had seen the foundation of Cheboksary, which was to become the Chuvash capital. In 1551, Chuvash and Mari envoys went to Moscow, to ask Tsar Ivan IV (the Terrible) to take their peoples into the Russian state. This year was thus a crucial date for the Chuvash, linking their fate permanently with that of Russia. When Kazan was taken by Russia in 1555, Chuvash troops were fighting alongside the Russians. Since that time, all important events in the life of the Chuvash have been indissolubly linked with the history of Russia. This history is well known, and needs no comment here, save to remark that the participation of many Chuvash in the risings of Stenka Razin and Pugachov left a considerable mark on Chuvash oral poetry.

The social and economic life of the Chuvash in Tsarist Russia was much like that of other non-Russian peoples. It is worth noting, however, that about four-fifths of the population was made up of *state peasants*, who worked individual holdings, the forests, pasture lands, lakes and rivers being given over to common use. There was almost no personal serf-owning in Chuvashia. But the way in which the people were exploited by the Russian authorities is eloquently indicated by the revolutionary Russian writer Herzen: 'The police and civil servants do unbelievable things to these poor folk.'

The Christianization of the Chuvash, which began in the sixteenth century, proceeded very slowly, with no open administrative pressure; the old religion was allowed to persist. In the 1740s, however, armed force began to be used;

the people were driven to the lakes and rivers to undergo mass baptism. In the space of ten years, the activities of the 'Conversion Office' resulted in the baptism of nearly all the Chuvash. Until the 1930s there remained about 2% of 'pagans'; over the centuries this stubborn minority kept up the struggle for their rites and customs. But those who had been christened long remained pagan in their everyday life and its secret essentials, which were hidden from the prying eyes of civil servants and clergy.

('Chuvash song was a "song from the ravine"', wrote Kheveder Pavlov, the founder of professional Chuvash music, 'because the working people, suffering from an oppressive yoke, did not dare to settle in open places, on the wide fields, by the highroads. Like wild beasts terrorized by the hunt, they went to earth in the dark ravines. In those days the Chuvash language was mocked and Chuvash song was laughed at. So they did not dare sing loudly and clearly in front of other peoples. In Chuvash villages it was only at night that you could hear from the ravines the sad songs of girls celebrating some festival' . . .)

Shortly after the union of the Central Volga with Russia there were the first attempts to give the 'aliens' a 'civilized' education; two 'alien' schools were opened in the sixteenth century by Archbishop Gury of Kazan. In the eighteenth century over 500 Chuvash children passed through the 'new converts' schools'. In the early nineteenth century about sixty schools were opened for Chuvash children; teaching was in Russian. Children were brought by force to these schools, in which their native language, customs and habits were ignored. 'It is not surprising,' writes a Chuvash ethnographer, 'that the Chuvash spared nothing – neither money, nor bread, nor honey – to save their children from attending these schools . . . And the children had only one way of avoiding them – to run away.'

Russification had been the order of the day, but in the 1860s, after a lengthy debate about the problems of educating the non-Russian peoples along the Volga, the so-called Ilminsky system was adopted. Professor N. I. Ilminsky, the Russian orientalist, considered it necessary for these peoples to be taught in their own languages, by teachers who came from their midst. The system was, in certain respects, a two-edged weapon. On the one hand, the development of their culture on a Christian basis brought the Chuvash ever closer to the Russians. At the same time, the understanding of the essence of Christianity and of the foundations of the European world view, which came to them, by way of translation, in their own language, led to the establishing of a Chuvash literary language and the appearance of a genuinely Chuvash literature which was founded on the ancient ethical and aesthetic values of the people.

The adoption of the Ilminsky system meant of course that it was necessary to create as quickly as possible a system of writing for the peoples of the Volga. The previous hundred years had seen the first beginnings of Chuvash literature, but during this time, because there was no Chuvash alphabet, Chuvash words had to be transcribed in Russian characters. This was a serious obstacle to the development and extension of writing in Chuvash. This obstacle was overcome and the education of the Chuvash people became a truly national undertaking with the appearance of the great figure of Ivan Yakovlevich Yakovlev (1848–1930), of whom Lenin, who knew the 'patriarch of Chuvash culture' from childhood, said that he possessed a 'heroic spirit'. Thanks to his unflagging labours, a Chuvash school, which can be called the first genuinely national Chuvash university, came into being.

Yakovlev was born in the village of Kanna-Kushki, in the Teche district of Tataria; an illegitimate child, he was left an orphan when his mother died a few days after his birth. In his childhood he worked as a shepherd, and was forcibly enrolled in the village school, one of the Russian schools which the people called 'houses of death'. He was already an adult by the time he graduated from the *gymnasium* in Simbirsk; while he was still a student there, in 1868, he opened a school for Chuvash children in his little room. He went out to persuade children to come to this school and paid for their transport, their keep and their tuition from the small sum of money he had saved up while working as a surveyor.

The school began with one pupil. Then Yakovlev managed to enrol a second, a third, a fourth . . . In his old age, he recalled sadly how he lost his fourth pupil: 'He ran away back home to his village, being homesick and unable to get used to town life. Try as I might, I could not overcome this feeling of his. I took him for walks in the parks and the outskirts of the town, but in vain. I would take him to a forest, but he would say: "You call that a forest! We have real forests at home." So he pined away, and in the end he left me. He was a warm-hearted and sensitive boy.' So, a year after the founding of the school, he had three pupils.

When he went on to Kazan University at the age of 22, Yakovlev kept an eye on his school from a distance. He hired teachers for his pupils and collected money for the keep of teachers and pupils alike. While he was a student, it was I.N. Ulyanov, inspector of schools in the Simbirsk region and the father of Lenin, who helped run the school. And it was on his prompting that it was officially recognized by the Ministry of Education in 1871. In 1877 it was transformed into the Central Chuvash Seminary and received official authorization to train teachers for the Chuvash village schools.

I described the Simbirsk school as a genuine 'Chuvash university'. By 1875, when Yakovlev was appointed Inspector of Chuvash Schools for the Kazan district, it had become a centre of Chuvash culture. With students such as Kestenttin Ivanov, Nikolay Shubussini and Kheveder Pavlov, it was to give birth to the new Chuvash literature, to a genuinely national ethnography, and to Chuvash history, music and painting.

Here too the new Chuvash alphabet came into existence. It was created in 1871–2 by Yakovlev, who added to the Russian (Cyrillic) script a number of special symbols to denote specifically Chuvash sounds. He immediately began to publish books written in Chuvash, first the 'Yakovlev alphabet', which became a byword among the people, and also prayer books, popular science, textbooks, translations of Tolstoy's 'reading book' and of various works by Pushkin, Lermontov, and others. Above all, a complete translation of the Bible was made under Yakovlev's direction. It appeared just before the Revolution, and did not play such a large part in the development of the Chuvash literary language as the King James Bible in English or Luther's bible in German. Even so, one can detect the influence of the translation of the Gospels, which was published towards the end of the nineteenth century, in various half-pagan, half-Christian folk prayers, written down at the beginning of the twentieth century.

The foundation, the inexhaustible fountain head of Chuvash literature, ethnography and linguistics was the famous 'Dictionary of the Chuvash Language' of Nikolay

Ashmarin (1870–1933), who received a great deal of help in his work from Yakovlev and his pupils. His seventeen-volume dictionary contains a wealth of lexical material for the various dialects of the language, and the majority of words are accompanied by lengthy descriptions of the ancient Chuvash way of life, implements and other artefacts, and the mythology and traditions of the people. Both Russian scholars and Chuvash writers have called it the 'encyclopedia of Chuvash life'.

In this way, thanks to the work of Yakovlev and his many followers, the Chuvash language became in the pre-Revolutionary period the language of written literature, schoolroom instruction, church sermons and prayers – and in the years of the first Russian revolution the language of the press. In the words of Yakovlev's son, 'a literary language was created in a single generation, when other nations have needed centuries'. The basis of this language was the Lower Chuvash (*anatri*) dialect, which was 'purer' and less subject than Upper Chuvash to the influence of the Finno-Ugrian – and later, Russian, languages.

In 1903, in order to prevent the development of Chuvash 'national separatism', Yakovlev, whose work had received little official support, was removed from his post as inspector of schools and appointed inspector of the Chuvash Seminary in Simbirsk. Again in 1917, at a congress of the Chuvash National Society, the most radical of the nationalists tried to have him removed from his post as director of the Simbirsk school. Lenin intervened, sending a telegram to the president of the Simbirsk Soviet which said: '. . . I am concerned for the fate of Inspector Ivan Yakovlevich Yakovlev, who has worked for fifty years for the Chuvash cause and suffered much harassment from the Tsarist authorities. I do not consider that Yakovlev should be taken away from his life's work.' In our own day, representatives of the Chuvash intelligentsia in Moscow gather every spring at the Vagankov cemetery to remember the great enlightener, the 'grandfather of all the Chuvash'.

IV

A man may say many things to other people about his mother. He may cite events from her long-suffering life, or even describe in detail her spiritual and moral nature. But how can he convey that *circle of faintly-glowing light*, which is mysterious even to him, though he can see and feel it in himself without so much as naming his mother. This whole anthology is an attempt to convey to foreign readers something of that *circle of light*, which is in this case the spiritual and moral nature of the Chuvash people, faintly glowing behind all the texts printed here. I know, however, that not only in this anthology and its introduction, but even in the essence of my whole life, I can never 'describe' or convey the inexpressible radiance of my 'mother-people' (the Chuvash language has no category of gender, so that the people, the sun and the Volga can all be called 'father' or 'mother').

Many characteristics of the Chuvash are of course common to all peoples, and in particular to the small nations of the Volga. What, however, are the moral and psychological traits that particularly characterize the Chuvash? In the first place, what marks out the Chuvash in any company, and among any people, is their remarkable (almost 'religious') attitude of respect and veneration for old people, particularly for the oldest person present (see in this anthology the 'Guest Songs' and Okhotnikov's 'Festivals'). During my childhood, in the difficult wartime and postwar years, I several times saw men who were strong, well-to-do (for the times) and too big for their boots being put in their place by a poor, weak man, who was however the oldest person in the village.

The cult of elders involves a converse obligation; the Chuvash have a highly developed sense of paternal responsibility for any member of the younger generation. A related notion is that of the whole village as a single family – thus in the old days the 'Festival of the Name', when a name was given to a new-born child, was a festival for the whole village. The same was true of weddings and of various kinds of work. Even today, the whole village will gather for the *Nime*, when the community helps one individual with his or her work.

Next one must mention the extraordinary ritualism of the Chuvash. A Chuvash will ritually open someone else's gate (and close it behind him carefully, with the extreme respect due to the work of another hand), he will ritually open the door, wait ritually on the threshold, ritually greet the people of the house, wait for the ritual answer, ritually decline an invitation, ritually refuse to sit down. Thereafter, in the hour of conversation that follows, both host and guest will continue to observe the appropriate rituals, though this might not be obvious to an outsider. It would be wrong to equate this ritualism with superstition. Its main purpose (excepting a few clear cases of superstition) is the constant daily creation of a consciously charitable spirit of community among those who belong to the same group. It involves working attentively and unceasingly to consolidate this community spirit.

It is hard to find suitable words to evoke the tactfulness of the Chuvash. I remember the poet Khuzangay saying to me one day: 'There is no-one to bring you up, you children of the war. Most of you have no fathers, your mothers are out in the fields, the only hope is that your inborn Chuvash tact will save you.' One element in this tact, and a very important one in conversation, is indirectness. Its essence is summed up in the proverb: 'Tell your daughter, and your daughter-in-law will hear you'. Even in daily family life, the Chuvash try not to ask anyone directly for anything. They go round about. 'I think the girl has bought some tea', says a Chuvash to his wife, meaning simply: 'Let's have some tea'.

Some Russian ethnographers have written that the Chuvash are 'secretive and suspicious'. Gury Komissar-Vander replied to this in 1911: 'The Chuvash is naturally open-hearted and trusting. He is simple, sincere and kind. But experience has taught him not to trust everyone, and in his relations with strangers, particularly officials, he is often mistrustful and secretive . . . With a person whom he trusts and respects, he can be simple to the point of naivety, frank, open and affable . . . The Chuvash attaches himself to a good person like a child . . . He is peaceable and easy-going, but not particularly decisive, and very cautious in any new undertaking.'

Once in my youth, at a party with some Moscow artists, I was asked 'as a friend' to teach them some Chuvash swear-words. I could not think of any. This brings me to the question of modesty. There are all kinds of people in any community, but if we think of the Chuvash people as a whole, it must be said that in their life, their language and their folklore, immodesty is almost unknown. Yakovlev writes in his memoirs of his embarrassment as a Chuvash at a party of ex-students where obscene jokes were being told, and in another place notes: 'There is nothing shameful, disgusting or cynical in any Chuvash songs.' The lack of curses and swear-words in the Chuvash language is borne out by all the ethnographers and linguists.

In one of his poems the Chuvash poet Vasley Mitta gives a place among the good spirits and deities to Thrift and Moderation. Undoubtedly thrift is one of the specific qualities of the Chuvash. 'This is not miserliness, but economy', writes the ethnographer N.V. Nikolsky, 'wealth which is the fruit of long and patient labour should not be frittered away, but employed sensibly.'

One must also mention the bond between the Chuvash and the natural world. This is so close that often in Chuvash folklore it is hard to distinguish human beings and their feelings from plants, trees or forests. Nikolsky writes: 'If a Chuvash sees someone stripping the bark from a living tree, he will immediately say to him: "Why are you taking the bark off that tree; how would you like to have your skin taken off you?"' It is worth noting that it was considered a sin among the Chuvash to cut down old trees in a village – they had to be allowed to die a natural death, like old people. The Chuvash attitude to animals, plants and the whole natural world is well brought out in the text by Kerguri Timofeyev included below.

As far as the family life of the Chuvash is concerned, let me simply quote the celebrated Hungarian scholar A. Vambery: 'The Chuvash man behaves in a loving manner towards his wife and family . . . This way of behaving goes back to the past, for whereas the theology and mythology of the other Turkic peoples contain only male deities, the Chuvash in their pagan period also worshipped female deities. In all their games and customs, the women have the dominating role' (*Das Türkenvolk*, vol. III, Leipzig, 1885).

A lot was written in the years between 1920 and 1950 about the oppressed and well-nigh servile condition of Chuvash women. This is not the place to examine how this came about, or from what foreign sources these ideas were drawn. Let us listen, however, to the voice of Ivan Yakovlev: 'Among the Chuvash, who lead an exceptionally private, family-centred life, the woman occupies as important a position as the man, perhaps more important. She takes part with him in the work of the fields, is in charge of the home, brings up the children and has a prominent part in the pagan religious rituals. But as she takes such an active part in the life of the family, she hardly ever goes beyond the limits of her family and village.' In the Chuvash world view, the woman and mother was sacred and inviolable. 'The mother is a *kebe* (one of the highest deities), you must not insult her', says a Chuvash proverb.

When he read the 'Parents' Valediction to the Bride and Bridegroom' (reproduced in this anthology), one of my Ukrainian friends remarked: 'This little text is a powerful moral code; it says everything necessary for a decent human life. Sometimes small nations say things which are needed by large ones.' Let me therefore now quote in its entirety the 'Song of Gratitude' by G.N. Volkov, since this stresses several points in this unwritten 'moral code' of the Chuvash:

> *Answer a kind smile with a beautiful song,*
> *If you are told a proverb, reply with a tale,*
> *Answer a handshake with a firm embrace,*
> *If you are given milk, invite everyone to drink mead,*
> *If you are given mittens, give a black lamb,*
> *If they help you build a fence, help them build a house,*
> *To thank your mother for her care, bake her pancakes,*
> *Whoever helps you to your feet, give your life for them,*
> *If you are invited to a funeral, do not weep drunken tears,*
> *Rock the little orphans, sing them a cradle song.*

When a child was born to its mother *(kebe)*, they used immediately to perform a symbolic rite; they carved the umbilical cord on to the handle of the working tool of the father or mother. The cord of a boy was carved on to the handle of his father's scythe with the words 'Be like your father, a master of all trades'. The cord of a girl was carved on to the mother's distaff with the words 'Be hardworking like your mother, be a skilful worker'. Thus, from the first minutes of life, the future of the child was tied by blood to the life work of the father and mother, the working life of the whole people.

V

In 1908 Ivan Yakovlev published in Simbirsk the first anthology of Chuvash literature, 'Stories and Legends of the

Chuvash'. It included work by three major poets, Mikhail Fyodorov, Nikolay Shubussinni and Kestenttin Ivanov.

Fyodorov's ballad 'Arzyuri', written in 1879, circulated widely in manuscript before being published in Yakovlev's anthology. It introduced into Chuvash literature the foreign motif of a man wandering amidst the raging elements, which are personified as evil spirits. Such a theme is not to be found in Chuvash folklore; it appears to correspond to a strange impulse (on the part of a number of poets) towards the unconscious memory of some earlier period in Chuvash pagan belief – the spirits, once familiar, have become alienated from the people, and seem to demand that those who wander among them should recognize them.

The third of the poets mentioned above was to become the first and constant love of his people. Romantic in spirit and realistic in detail, his narrative poem *Narspi*, which tells the story of a Chuvash Romeo and Juliet, became the first classic of Chuvash literature. It is virtually impossible to convey through translation the quality of Ivanov's unique gift and the significance of his work, but if his quiet radiance could penetrate even faintly into the vision of the foreign reader, it would tell him something valuable about the spiritual nature of the Chuvash people.

Konstantin Vasilyevich Ivanov – *our Kestenttin* – was the first great Chuvash poet and dramatist, a master of poetic translation, the first significant Chuvash photographer, one of the first Chuvash ethnographer-historians, a folklorist, and an artist who venerated Leonardo da Vinci. When he returned to his native village from Simbirsk four months before his untimely death, he left behind him an unfinished wooden typewriter of his own invention. He also left unfinished a sculpted bust of his mother, the mother to whom he said as he lay dying: 'Mother, what a sunny dress you are wearing today. When I get well, I shall put on a shirt like that' (the sunny golden colour is central to *Narspi*). He died of tuberculosis in 1915, in the stone house which he had designed for his father; his creative work as a poet was already complete by 1908, when he was 18.

Most of Ivanov's poetic work, like that of other poets writing between 1900 and 1930, is written in lines of seven syllables. In this connection I should say a few words here about Chuvash prosody. Because Chuvash written poetry only began very recently, it is hard to tell what sources, other than oral folk poetry, are responsible for its formal features. The question is complicated by the fact that the classical literature of the Turkic languages, impregnated by the norms of Arabic and Persian poetry, influenced the oral poetry of the Turkic peoples, including those living in the Volga region. The Turkic seven-syllable line was widespread in folk poetry, and for several decades of Chuvash written poetry it dominated other metres. Longer lines of verse were much less common, though they were important in some types of oral poetry, in particular the guest songs.

It is in these guest songs that the outlook of the Chuvash is most clearly revealed. They are songs of the older generations, and they seem to contain the accumulated spiritual values of these generations, which are thus passed on, suitably modified in each period, to the succeeding generations as the immortal and all-embracing testament of the people. For these and similar songs, sung at the collective winter festivals, lines of nine, ten and eleven lines were normal.

(The most important of all the guest songs was the one entitled 'Alran kaimi' – 'Inseparable from us' – which was like the traditional hymn of the Chuvash people. This majestic song was always performed in a ritual manner. Before it was begun, an embroidered cloth was hung up by the family hearth; this 'domestic flag' was passed down from generation to generation. The song was sung by the older men, sitting at the table with beakers of beer in their hands, while the rest knelt in front of them with reverently bowed heads. Often, the song was repeated three times, and in some regions three youths would stand in front of the old men, moving their bodies to represent the waving corn. The performance was a special kind of oath of allegiance to popular traditions. The reverent attitude to it was such that the famous folk-singer Kaverle Fyodorov refused to sing it for composers to record, saying: 'It can't be sung like that.')

Nevertheless, the excellence of Ivanov's *Narspi* firmly established the seven-syllable line in Chuvash poetry. Firmly, but not for long. One year after his death, a seventeen-year old boy, the pupil of a religious village school, wrote his first poem. This was the beginning of the career of the most striking of all Chuvash poets.

Before the appearance of Mikhail Sespel (1899–1922),

Chuvash poetry seemed incapable of producing such a writer. Only some 'additional element' (to use Malevich's expression) can explain the great revolution in Chuvash poetry brought about by this poet who died before reaching the age of 23. In my view, this element can only be Sespel's genius. By a process of profound intuition, he worked out the stress patterns of the Chuvash language and used them as the basis for a syllabo-tonic prosody, which took the place of the preceding, purely syllabic system. This revolution brought Chuvash poetry much closer to Russian poetry, and thus to world poetry, allowing it to take in the latest poetic innovations of European literature. Words in Sespel's writing took on both a 'Futurist' texture and an 'Impressionist' radiance; he brought into Chuvash poetry images whose psycho-physiological individuality was previously unthinkable.

The Russian Revolution of 1917 had a huge impact on Sespel. He might have called it with Mayakovsky 'my Revolution'. It meant for him the hope of transforming the entire life of the Chuvash people and 'resurrecting his native tongue': 'The Chuvash language will cut through iron. It will grow sharp, will be red-hot steel'. The Chuvash scholar Atner Khuzangay remarks that Sespel 'plays the part of the demiurge, the creator of a world, accomplishing a cosmogonic act'. His poetry reworks many elements in ancient Chuvash mythology; for instance, he alludes to the magical function of metals, describing himself as a poet of 'steel faith' in the imminent rebirth of his native land. The theme of the previous humiliation and suffering of his people is developed in a number of his poems through a parallel with Golgotha.

Of all the inheritors of Sespel's 'steel faith', one must first mention Peder Khuzangay (1907–1970). A poet of wide culture, possessing a great sense of measure and a Verlainian gift for music, Khuzangay successfully brought into Chuvash literature many genres and forms from European poetry. Thanks to him, the melody of Chuvash poetry acquired a more European character. At the same time, he is the author of a genuinely national masterpiece, the 'Songs of Tilli', a cycle of poems on themes from folklore, each of which is a key to some important aspects of the traditional Chuvash world view.

To conclude this brief survey, let me turn to another major

poet, and one whose image is very dear to me, Vasley Mitta (1908–1957). I can best characterize him by drawing on an interview I gave to a Polish newspaper in 1974. 'Our most spiritually gifted poets', I said, 'are like peasants in their closeness to nature and its various manifestations; the best images of our poetry strike one by the peasant's attention to the detail of the physical world and by the ability to convey feelings which are not just the passions of the individual poet, but unite him fraternally with all men and with the entire people. The Chuvash have never known an elite culture; the intelligentsia which came into existence in the first half of the nineteenth century never had to face the agonizing question of its separation from the people; it served the people in a practical way, and in the most difficult circumstances.'

Fraternity was Mitta's favourite word. His own fate was extremely dramatic; he spent 17 years in the labour camps, in prison and in exile on the strength of an unfounded accusation and died at the age of 49. The tragic content of his poetry is very great, but even so, his poems show an amazing modesty; speaking of the most profound experiences of his time, the poet never talks of himself in particular – his words could be spoken by any ordinary person. Yet he by no means loses his individuality; in his best poems one can always hear his quiet voice, his calm, 'Socratic' intonation. Indeed, in everything he wrote or did there was something Socratic – a modest, laconic, but beautifully poetic reminder of very ancient and precious elements in Chuvash ethics and aesthetics. In his modest way, he left a brotherly testament to his compatriots. I too can hear the words he addressed to me: 'Your road will be a long one; remember the world is not a smooth road, do not stumble'.

VI

'May the centre of Cheboksary, in a burning flash of lightning, become a hearth radiating the fire of the New Word', wrote Mikhail Sespel in July 1921, far from his native land, at the height of the tragic Volga famine. On 25 April 1925, the Presidium of the All-Russian Central Executive Committee decreed that the Chuvash Autonomous Region, which had been created in 1920, should become the Chuvash Autonomous Socialist Republic within the RSFSR. Soviet power gave an enormous impulse to the renewal of Chuvash culture which Sespel in expectation had called the Rebirth of his Native Land, the Resurrection of the Chuvash Word.

The first years of the new power saw the establishment of a broad material base for the development of Chuvash national culture. A simple enumeration of facts bears witness to this. In Cheboksary, where before the Revolution there was not a single secondary school, there is now the Chuvash State University, two other establishments of higher education, two scientific research institutes, five theatres, a music school, three museums and the Chuvash art gallery. The state press publishes more books each year than were published in all the years before the Revolution. In 1970, to celebrate its half-century, this press issued 295 titles, with a total of 2,400,000 volumes (poetry is printed in editions of between 1,000 and 10,000).

Chuvashia has become one of the more highly developed industrial regions of the USSR, the two biggest enterprises being the Cheboksary heavy tractor factory and the hydro-electric power station on the Volga. It is not easy to make known abroad the economic and cultural achievements of small nations such as the Chuvash. Probably many people throughout the world first heard of them when the Chuvash cosmonaut Andriyan Nikolayev was put into space in August 1962. Let me therefore mention one or two names which should be known to readers of this anthology.

The most outstanding son of the Chuvash people in all their history is Iakinf Bichurin (1777–1853), the world famous sinologist, who has become a classic of Russian oriental studies. In more modern times one should mention the names of the Turkologist Vasily Yegorov (1880–1974) and the contemporary linguist Mikhail Fedotov and historian Vasily Kakhovsky. In the field of painting, Western art lovers would find the work of Anatoly Mittov (1932–1971) very interesting. His paintings convey the specific qualities of Chuvash life and landscape in a genuine and original way which recalls the work of such painters as the Georgian Piromanashvili, the Pole Nikifor Krynicki and the Hungarian Tivadar Csontváry.

The peoples of the Volga region occupy a special place among the many nationalities of the Soviet Union. They are composed of three Finno-Ugrian peoples (the Mari, the Udmurts and the Mordovians) and three Turkic ones (the Chuvash, the Tatars and the Bashkirs). This is a 'particular Russia' which still shows traces of the high culture of Greater Bulgaria, the first state to exist on the banks of the Volga. In publishing a Chuvash anthology, I should like to express the hope that readers throughout the world will also become acquainted with the other peoples of the Volga, whose inner world is best represented in poetry by the Tatars Gabdulla Tukey (1886–1913) and Khadi Taktash (1900–1930) and the Bashkirs Sheykhzada Babich (1895–1919) and Mustay Karim (born 1919).

Finally let me emphasize that in this introduction I have not quoted any of the scornful, belittling comments on the Chuvash, their language and their poetry which are so common in the eighteenth and nineteenth century. It seems to me that there has been enough copying of these remarks from one book to another. However, I have decided to quote just one anonymous comment to represent all this cheap talk, an anonymous writer of 1828 who expressed the view that the Chuvash 'are incapable of producing anything worthy of man's higher nature'. I shall not answer this connoisseur of 'man's higher nature' myself, but entrust the task to an eminent Russian writer.

As I finish this work, which has taken me more than ten years, I want to take one final look at the collective face of my people. In a sense I (who am one flesh and blood with this people), as I take my leave of this book, am also taking leave of this face, its eternity and its abiding past. I open the pages of a book of sketches by N.G. Garin-Mikhailovsky, 'The Bustle of Provincial Life', published in 1900. I hear the ringing of the metallic head-dresses, the Chuvash *tevet*. The meadow is bathed in 'unendurably ancient light' (to quote another writer). Through the eyes of a Russian observer, I see the Festival of my people, its youth which will live as long as Chuvash and the Chuvash word:

> *Once, not long after sowing time, I came across their spring festival "Uyav", in honour of Tura and of a young goddess, the daughter of the great and good Tura.*
> *On a cheerful meadow there were young men and girls dancing in a ring. The girls were wearing a kind of long, white*

blouse, embroidered with red calico, with red belts and a sort of tail hanging down; they had strange head-dresses, metal caps like those worn by ancient warriors in the days of Prince Vladimir, with a point on the crown of the head; long bands of cloth were hanging from their caps over their breasts and cheeks, and on these were sewn large and small silver coins.

Dressed like this, the girls looked fresh and strange, like something out of a fairy tale.

– Can I buy a hat? – I asked.

– You can't buy them, but you can look at them, – replied an old man who was interpreting for me.

He went over to the girls and tried to persuade them to come closer. At first they were reluctant, but eventually they came.

I watched how they walked: calmly, confidently, gracefully.

– Look, – said the old man.

Coming up to me, the girls joined hands, made a big circle and began to sing; there was something extremely original about their singing; and it was a sight such as I had never seen before. Or rather I had seen it, but on the stage, in ballet or opera. But this was not a ballet or opera, it was life.

The big circle went round smoothly and slowly; the girls walked one behind the other, turning sideways. They took one large stride, stopped and then gently brought the other foot forward.

On the stage it might have seemed artificial; here this choral dance of young Vestals was natural and inexpressibly beautiful.

They looked straight in front of them and sang.

– What are they singing about?

– They are singing without words, – answered the old man, – this song can only be sung once a year, no more. This is how they will sing when they go to Tura after they die. They will look him in the eyes and will go forward singing . . . singing, but without words.

The old man talked, and I listened to him.

Sometimes the sound of the singing grew loud in the fragrant meadows and rose into the sky, mingling with the singing of a lark, a quiet sweet song of times past.

What are operas and romances? Can they convey that fragrance of eternally youthful spring and tender sorrow for passing time? Can they convey that song of the people, who have carried with them through the wreckage of the years this bright image of their former life? Can such a song be invented?

The girls had finished dancing and they were gazing at me,
still enveloped in their own song.

* * *

In compiling this anthology, I encountered many difficulties
which need not be mentioned here. Suffice it to say that some
of the early religious texts had to be reconstructed; in some
cases I had dozens of variants for a single text, and in using
them I followed strictly the recommendations of Chuvash,
Hungarian and Finnish scholars. Certain lengthy texts by
poets of undoubted talent had to be abridged, but this only
concerns one or two of the more recent authors. Being
concerned essentially with the established body of Chuvash
poetry, this anthology does not include the work of any poets
born after 1930, but the Epilogue indicates some recent
developments.*

Recalling that my work on this volume was done without
support from official Chuvash organizations, I must express
my special fraternal gratitude to the Chuvash poet, scholar
and folklorist Gennady Yumart (whose help made him on
occasions a co-author) and to the linguist and literary scholar
Atner Khuzangay. To them both I say thank you – *tav*.

Gennady Aygi
Moscow, April 1982

* *Today, over eight years on, it seems appropriate to add to the anthology a*
further eight poets, including two who are discussed in the epilogue.
G.A., October 1991

I.

*Texts Associated with
the Ancient Pagan Mythology
of the Chuvash People*

Midwife's address to the child after washing

You have come out from your own place,
now look on the world from your new place,
live till you are old and weak,
live till you are feeble in mind,
be happy, as we are happy.
Honour me in my old age.
When your mother was weak
and could not care for you,
I came at your weeping
and took you in my arms.
I washed your bottom, baby,
when your mother could not.
Honour me and respect me in time to come.

Prayer at the festival of the name
(when the child's name is confirmed)

Oh Tura!
We give this child a name,
We give him the name 'Attil'.
Let him have Thy grace;
may he walk behind the plough;
may be live like us till he is old and weak,
till he loses his reason,
till he begins to put shoes on back to front.
When he meets an elder, let him say 'Tede',
when he meets a young man, let him say 'Brother';
may he care for his father and mother,
may our race be budded on
from him in the future,
may our race continue from age to age.
Ours to grow old,
ours to leave this world,
may he have our blessing;
Thou also, bless him,
Oh Tura!

(*Tede* – respectful form of address to an elder)

4

Prayer of the priest or prayer leader at the field prayers of the whole people known as 'Uidyuk'

Most high Tura,
have mercy!

We come to the Field Sacrifice;

with living sacrifices,
with warm faces, with sweet lips
we stand before Thee to pray;
with the whole people, with the whole world
we bow down before Thee, we are comforted;

shedding blood,
ending lives of souls,
we ask Thy protection
for our three kinds of cattle,
for our seven kinds of corn;
do not parch Thy Earth,
save from Fire, from Hail, from Enemy Water;
grant us to gather for one grain a thousand,
may the stems of corn be like reeds,
may the ears be like heads of bullrushes,
may the grains be big as peas;
may our mares be followed
by their foals,
our cows by calves;

send us needy guests:
may we warm the frozen,
and feed the hungry;

forgive us, Tura,
if by thoughtless words we have sinned
before one another, before our cattle,
before any creature.

Send thy grace to the labouring people,
Oh Tura!

Ploughman's prayer

Oh Father of the Earth,
Mother of the Earth!

Beyond the dark forest
with shouting and song
we plough and we sow;
four horses are ploughing,
a dun mare pulls the harrow,
and her foal runs behind her:
he frisks and plays, tears the cloth with the grain,
eats and scatters it on the ground.

Father of the Earth,
Mother of the Earth,
Family of the Earth!
Give strength to the horses, creatures without speech;
and bestow abundance
of seed in the hand
and seed in the basket!
Send down dew in its season,
and let us rejoice
at the sight of green shoots!

Father of the Earth,
Mother of the Earth!
We Chuvash have no writing,
all that we can do
is bow and beseech you
with sweet mouths and warm hearts:

Oh Gods, have mercy!

Prayer of the sower

Rye,
with the help of Tura,
be rival of the forest!
In heavy earth, on dark days,
be active and grow,
as buds burst in the forest!
I dip my dusty cap in the spring
and as I see it washed clean,
even so may my soul
be purged of filth
before you,
Oh Rye!

Prayer at the festival of sacrificial beer offering

(The invocations of the gods are spoken in turn by the master of the house and the guests of honour, the prayer itself is spoken by the priest or the oldest man present)

- Oh Tura, Oh Piulekh;
- Mother of Tura, Mother of Piulekh, Spirit who abidest
     before Tura;
- Anger of Tura, Sufferings of Tura, Sickness of Tura,
     Misfortunes of Tura;
- Kebe, Pikhamber, Wayfaring Spirit, Khrban,
     Gates of Heaven, World of the Here;
- Father of the Sun, Mother of the Sun, Wings of the Sun,
     Feet of the Sun, Ears of the Sun, Anger of the Sun,
     Sufferings of the Sun, Sickness of the Sun,
     Misfortunes of the Sun;
- Father of the Wind, Mother of the Wind,
     Wings of the Wind, Anger of the Wind, Sufferings of
     the Wind, Sickness of the Wind, Misfortunes of
     the Wind, Guardian of the Wind;
- Lord of the Earth, Father of the Earth, Mother of the Earth,
     Body of the Earth, Family of the Earth, Yusman,
     who abidest before the Possessor of the Earth,
     Anger of the Earth, Sufferings of the Earth,
     Sickness of the Earth, Misfortunes of the Earth,
     Exhalation of the Earth;
- Father of the Water, Mother of the Water, Red Bank,
     Mother of the Bright Lake:
- Orderer of Earth and Water, Creator of the House,
     Giver of Bread, Giver of Children;
- Foundation of the House, Wealth of the Homestead,
     Wealth of the Granary, Shepherd of the Homestead,
     Protector of the Barn;
- Founder of Corn, Grower of Corn, Spirit that sways the corn;
- Father of Thrift, Mother of Thrift;
- Foundation of Animals, Protector of Cattle;
- Giver of bees, Maker of the movement of bees;
- Father of Flowers, Mother of Flowers;
- Begetter of Sweet, Begetter of Bitter;
- Fellow-traveller on the road, Guardian of the Ways,

Holder of the Reins, Suffering of the Traveller;
– Dweller in Bilyar, Dweller in Kazan;
– Kiremet Kebe, Great Kiremet, Little Kiremet, –

– Gods, have mercy!
Today I
with my children, my household,
with my family, my neighbour-guests,
with the village society,
with the whole people
come to stand before you
in joy, in inspiration
with sacrificial beer,
with the new corn;
turning to you with thanks
we proceed
to the tapping of the barrel.

Oh Tura!
Give wealth, give health!
For the new corn I thank thee, I bow low:
for one grain that is sown
give a thousand grains.
Guard us from future sufferings,
misfortunes, thieves, fires.
When we sail on the great water,
save from the breaking oar,
from the great wave, the rocking boat.
Grant us, Oh Tura,
to warm the traveller who comes frozen,
to send the hungry man on his way well fed!
Three kinds of corn
may we store in three granaries;
three kinds of cattle
and three homesteads give us;
let any feather, let any bird's down
be good to pay our debts.
The new-born cattle
may we guard with good hands
and bring forth the unborn!
Give the mare a foal, give the cow a calf,
may the cattle multiply

9

a thousand fold,
may one end of the herd be in the stockyard
and the other end by the pond,
and may they walk uninterrupted
one behind the other, neck to neck.
Give safe life to children of both kinds,
add soul to soul,
add house to house.
Make us glad with wealth,
give it even from the earth,
give it even from above,
may milled flour be never-ending,
may bought salt be never-ending.
Let the place whence it comes remain unseen,
in the place of its keeping let it not fail.

Oh Piulekh!
grant us to go evenly in thy ways,
to go chaste and untouched!
Help us on the way
to the meeting with goodness,
turn us from evil.
Let the work of the fields
be heart-felt,
and the work of the house
be seemly and quiet.

Oh God Pikhamber,
tame the wolf, thy dog,
let him not destroy our beasts!

Great God, Order of the Dead,
multiply the cattle
like the hair upon them!

God of the Cartshafts, have mercy,
do not take away our shafts!

Oh Father of the Earth, Mother of the Earth!
We talk too much of you,
we speak too many words
that are needless and misplaced!
Gods, have mercy!

Praise to the Father and Mother of Wind,
to their contagious spreading
in the wake of the storm from many lands.
Praise to the Father and Mother of Earth,
To her exhalations, which spread
all manner of harmful contagion.

Oh, Father of Wind, Mother of Wind!
Send your storms
less angrily.
May my house stand untouched a thousand years,
founded with zeal.

Oh, Father of Fire, Mother of Fire!
Less irresistibly
send your flame –
there is no life if we cannot keep
your fire in our hands,
this you have ordained for ever,
let it be so!

Oh heavenly Powers,
send down to us your Spirit,
your Breath!

Oh Gods!
We your simple children
perhaps said too late
what we should have said in the beginning,
and perhaps at the beginning
what we should have ended with, –
Gods have mercy on us!

Oh Tura,
may what is lacking
be filled up from this beaker!

Proclamation by the priest of the beginning of 'Sinze', the pregnancy of the earth

In the name of Tura
I proclaim Sinze!
It is forbidden
to knock, to pluck grass,
to heat the bathhouse, dry grain, thresh and grind;
it is forbidden
to dig the Earth, to take stones from Her;
it is forbidden to wear shirts and dresses
that are red or bright-coloured!
Let all be in white!

Bee prayer

Master of the house
Oh Tura, have mercy!
For the six-legged bees
I have made sweet mead,
assembled my household, my neighbours,
called together the whole village company,
assembled the whole people,
and I broach a cask of beer
sweetened with honey, –
let us pray to the Gods!

Old men (addressing the gods in turn)
– Kebe, Mother of Bees;
– Bee Gods; God of Swallows;
– God of Woodpeckers;
– God of Wrens;
– God of Nightingales!
– World of Light;
– Gates of Heaven;
– Wayfaring Spirit;
– Breath of God!

Priest – Prayer Leader
Gods, have mercy!
Tura, have mercy!
Give this householder the grace
to have his fill of sweet honey and sweet mead!
To the whole village company,
to neighbours and guests,
to a thousand people – beginning with the first –
give fullness!
Let one end of the bees
be on the flowers,
and the other end
in a swarm in the hives!
May there be enough to feed
the hungry traveller
and send him honourably on his way!
Give your grace, Gods,
give unending plenty!

Prayer to the Spirit of the Field
before harvest

(In the field all the members of the family stand in a row facing
the East. The oldest cuts a few stalks with his sickle, throws them
in front of him and speaks the prayer)

Oh, Spirit of the Field!
Give me thy strength,
make my waist strong and supple,
and my fingers firm;
let me be glad, looking forward,
at the swaying richness,
and looking backward, at the abundance of stooks.

Oh, Father of the Earth!
I have entered this field
like the wind;
help me to leave it
like the storm!
May others see my entering,
but may my departing
remain unnoticed.
Father,
have mercy!

14

Song before the conclusion of the Autumn Sacrifice

For milking – a white cow,
For saddling – a bay horse,
For hospitality – our fathers' house
To last down the centuries.

I have cut a whole birch for a cabin,
I have made a road to the river.
The strength this work has given me
I have offered my people in hospitality.

Rain drips: *shibr, shibr, –*
Let us go in beneath the birches.
Let us fall down before the elders
At the table beneath their feet.

Prayer to water

Father of Water, Mother of Water,
have mercy!

Water, have mercy!
I bow before thee, I bow down low.
Whether my soul was frightened
when I crossed you by night,
or by day you sent fear
or frightened my children,
or whether in anger I struck my cattle
or cursed my horse,
be merciful,
receive my offerings,
have mercy!

Incantation for fermenting beer

With the help of Tura,
Mother of Water and Fire,
be playful as lightning,
as waters in spring!

To work, more quickly,
to work!
Honoured guests await thee,
the people await!

As a white steed is saddled
and on a white felt
a white bird pursued,
even so, seethe up,
to work!

Prayer of the musician who plays the shabar at a feast

Oh, Tura!
With thy blessing let us travel roads of milk,
and return on roads of butter.
Someone maybe
will want to spoil our rejoicing.
Let him only defeat us
when he can stand full height
at the highest table
of the most high Tura.
Bless us,
oh Tura!

(*shabar* – a sort of bagpipe)

Offering a ritual doll to the Spirit of the Lake

Lake,
have mercy on Sarnebi!
Perhaps it was you
who sent disease upon her.
Here is body for body
here is face for face
here is bone for bone.
Leave Sarnebi in peace!

Charm for the shedding of blood

(spoken while placing a metal object on the wound)

Oh, Gods!

It is the Daughter's Father
who cuts and wounds,
it is not I.
And the Daughter sows it up.
With a red thread
she sews a red seam.
The seam is sewn – the blood is staunched.

The dancing beaker

(Words of gratitude of the guest who has been given the 'dancing beaker', after which he must dance)

Thanks to you and gratitude,
dancing beaker,
beaker with my name from a host who is kind!
In the heavens is Tura,
on earth the Tsar!
Let there be such barley
that a horse could not drag it,
let there be such hops
that no hand could lift them!
He who drains this beaker is a quail,
he who does not is a corncrake.
If I do not drain it,
may I lie alone,
apart from my loved one.

Prayer before entering the bath house

Oh, Mother-Fire!
Sit quietly on your cushion,
do not play, be at rest.
Let forty women wash themselves
and fifty men.
Let me after the bath ride round the village
on a two-year-old colt!
Wash the men on their crowns,
the women on their middle parts,
the girls on their sides!
Let heat remain in the bath house
while in the village strength remains
in the tireless body
of the last loose woman!

Bathing prayer

Tura, have mercy,
send down your help!

May this bath
be like honey, like butter.
Louse be eaten by louse,
nit be eaten by nit,
flea be eaten by flea.

I shall lie down to sleep –
may my sleep be peaceful,
may I rise from my bed
in one jump, like a flea,
ikh, ikh, ikh!

Prayer to Khertsurt,
Goddess of the Hearth

Oh, Khertsurt!

Give us who live in one house with you
joyful gatherings
and sweet conversation.
Give a bride for the bedchamber,
a son-in-law in the doorway.
Be the Mother of the House!
Sitting on your stove
on a soft cushion,
preserve order and peace
in our house!

Khertsurt,
have mercy!

Snake charm

(spell against estrangement)

Tura, be merciful!

Wrathful Esperuk moves and hisses;
the snake writhes and stretches;
I make a spell for this man
against his estrangement, his coldness, –
from his place of the snake,
from the place where he hisses like a snake,
I drive out his estrangement, his coldness to near ones,
I come to this task
With the Mother of Tura;
the snake writhes, stretches and plays –
let the man's eyes too be sad
and fill with longing,
may his soul come to life,
his heart be softened.

Tura, be merciful! Send down thy grace!

At the back of the threshing floor is a black snake,
he wants to crawl out to the middle,
he writhes, stretches, shudders, and frets, –
so too in the eyes of the man
may the warmth of kindness appear
and his soul be washed, made pure,
and may the Hour of God return,
may his Power work again!

In the middle of the four-cornered four-sided Universe
the glance of the Sun appears,
the Sun expands,
the World is lit,
the Earth is warmed, –
so too may the man's eyes grow warm
and into his washed soul
come kindness.

And may the Hour of God return to him!

The snake writhes, slides away,
he twists, he returns,
so too may the Hour of God return,
His active Power!
To the answer to my prayers
I listened with the Mother of God,

let goodness come also from me,
Tura, and protect me,
be merciful!

Spell for separating lovers

When the Lord of the Graveyard
unites seventy-seven skulls
from seventy-seven graveyards
in one single skull,
only then let Palastai
be united with Ilembi.

When the seventy-seven tails
of seventy-seven branching roads
are united in one road,
only then let Palastai
be united with Ilembi,

When the Guardian of seventy-seven woods
unites all the treetops of those woods
in one single treetop,
only then let Palastai
be united with Ilembi.

When Palastai and Ilembi
carry earth of seventy-seven kinds
from the graves of seventy-seven graveyards,
only then let them
be united.

Albasta
(exorcism of Albasta, spirit of evil)

Albasta of the wind, Albasta of treasures, Albasta of water, Albasta of fire, Fiery Khayar, Fiery Sekhmet – goes away, goes back to his place, because fiery Uzal approaches him.

Day comes back, – may you too go back to your place, earth comes back – go back, sun comes back – go back, moon comes back – go back. Let him who came by the road depart by the road, him who came by water depart by water, him who came with the wind depart with the wind, him who came up to the face depart from the face, him who came up to the body depart from the body, him who settled in the body go out of the body. From man comes goodness, from God comes grace. Go, go, go. All things go back, you too go back.

Albasta of the dog, Albasta of the hen, Albasta of the bird, Albasta of the bath house, Vubor of the wind, Vubor of the sun, Vubor of the water, Vubor of the dead bird, Vubor of money, fiery Vubor, Fiery Sekhmet, Fiery Khayar – goes away, back to his place because fiery Uzal approaches him.

Day returns, – may You too go back, earth returns – go back.

Between Kiev and Moscow is a girl of twelve, – go to her, do not quarrel, do not argue.

Iron charm

Seventy-seven times there is dawn, rising and growing red, – when blood at last flows from this dawn at the blow of an axe, only then let Khunadi's blood appear. I spit and I blow, may she be cured at once. From man comes goodness, from God comes grace.

Seventy-seven times there is a star, rising and growing white, – when blood at last flows from this star at the blow of an axe, only then let Khunadi's blood appear. I spit and I blow, may she be cured at once. From man comes goodness, from God comes grace.

Seventy-seven times there is the sun, rising and growing red, – when blood at last flows from this sun at the blow of an axe, only then let Khunadi's blood appear. I spit and I blow, may she be cured at once. From man comes goodness, from God comes grace.

Charm against stomach ache

One two three four five six seven eight nine ten eleven;

may Uzal's power be split into eleven:

one two three four five six seven eight nine
one two three four five six seven
one two three four five
one two three
one.

And let one
be taken
from one.

Taking leave from the departed
after the 'Yuba' funeral feast

Savander,
come here.
Here is a chair for you, go on to it.
Here is a bridge for you – from chair to table.
Go up, Savander, on to the table.
Farewell, Savander,
from this table
go forth to Tura.

Address to the departed on the Evening of the Great Candle, with sacrificial offering of the 'Autumn Beer'

Adakai,
do not fear, come in.
Be with us a while.
Look at this light and remember,
and go forth with this memory.
Bless your house, your father and mother, all your family,
the household cattle.
Then bless the village.
Bless me: I bore you and reared you.
I light a candle to you.
See what you have come to,
this is all that remains of you.
Adakai,
I have thrown you a piece of wood there,
make a sledge, ride upon it.
Be married there.
But now go forth, Adakai,
never come again.

Conversation of the departed with Tura

(Not spoken by anyone, but an unspoken part of the ritual. The dead person is specially prepared for this imaginary conversation; a pearl and an agate are placed in the mouth, the eyes covered with silk and the ears too stopped with silk)

Tura
You said many unkind things of people,
you sinned greatly by slander.

Dead person
No, I did not open my mouth, I did not slander –
look, in my mouth is a pearl. I was silent.
I quarrelled with no-one – look, in my mouth is an agate.

Tura
Why did you not learn goodness?
Why did you not read the books that teach goodness?

Dead person
They did not teach me to read,
my eyes could not see –
look, my eyes are covered with silk.

Tura
Why did you not listen to the words of those
who teach of God?

Dead person
They stopped my ears with silk,
that is why I could not hear their words.

Conversation of the departed with Esrel, Lord of the Graveyard

Esrel
Is someone else still to come to the graveyard?

Dead person
I did not see – my eyes were stopped.

Esrel
But did you not hear about it?

Dead person
I did not hear – my ears were blocked.

Esrel
And did you smell no smell?

Dead person
No – my nose was covered.

Esrel
Why did you not ask anyone?

Dead person
My mouth also was stopped.

II.

Songs and speeches

Inseparable from us
(Drinking song)

Inseparable from us are plough and ploughshare,
Unforgettable our father and mother;
We shall not be separated from plough and ploughshare,
We shall not forget our father and mother.
Unforgettable are our kinsfolk and friends,
Dear neighbours and people of our village,
Let us drink and be happy together,
Live in friendship and harmony until we die.

Song of the Khan of Kazan before turning into a swan and flying away from his capital

(A song about the taking of Kazan by
Russian and Chuvash troops in 1552)

I fly away, I depart
To far places unknown to you;
Whoever comes with me
Will eat cake for bread;
Whoever stays behind
Will chew straw for bread;
Whoever flies with me
Will drink milk for water;
Whoever stays behind
For water
Will drink blood.

They slaughtered the black and white pig

They slaughtered the black and white pig,
And they laid the carcass on the table.
'Eat', they said – I would not eat,
Then they put a knife to my throat.
So the Russian god
Rose up against us,
To take away the faith
Of our fathers and forefathers.
But thank you – *rekhmet* –
To the Tsar of Russia:
In the faith of our forefathers
We are free to live . . .

Suddenly Stenka Razin

Down the Volga floats a carpet,
And on the carpet lies a corpse.
They tied up the carpet to the bank,
They harnessed a pair of horses,
They laid the corpse in a cart,
And carried it to the church.
The priest began the service,
And suddenly Stenka Razin
Raised his head and sat upright.

In the year of seventy three

In the year of seventy three,
In the month of February,
The town of Kazan, the hussars
Forced us to shout for help,
Forced us, forced us to shout for help.
They seized Pugach,
Ai, they took Pugach, they seized him,
Ai, they took him,
They seized him, they caught him, they bound him.
Ai, they seized Pugach,
Seized him, hung him on the cruel aspen,
On the very top.
Ai, Marusinnka wept
Black tears.
Do not weep, do not weep, Marusinnka,
We shall take you with us;
We shall take you,
Marusinnka, with us,
We shall call you,
Marusinnka, sister.
Ai, they took down Pugach
From the cruel aspen,
Ai, they placed Pugach
In an elm-wood hut,
Ai, they burnt Pugach
In the elm-wood hut,
They scattered his ash
In the open field.

(Concerns the Pugachev rising of 1773)

Emigrants' songs

I

We shall go, my brothers, to Istanbul,
And in a new place we shall build a new house.

In a new place we shall build a new house,
And in it three windows we shall make.

The first looks out on a garden,
And the second on the wide, wide steppe.

The second on the wide, wide steppe
And the third looks out to the sea.

Through the first one nightingales sing,
Through the second I see girls playing.

Through the second I see girls dancing,
Through the third the ships sail by.

The ships are on the waves, and I am in one,
They are aground, and I am aground on grief.

II

My father promised to build me a white house,
If pine trees grew up through the threshing floor.
Pine trees will hardly grow through the threshing floor,
My father will hardly build me a white house.
We shall have to go off to Siberia, brothers,
Fell pine trees in the deep woods and build houses.
When we have built houses in the deep woods,
Come and visit us brothers, come and see.

My sister promised to embroider me a towel,
If flax suddenly sprang up on the stove.
Flax will hardly spring up on the stove,
My sister will hardly embroider me a towel.
We shall have to go off to Siberia, brothers,
Sow flax and gather it in the deep woods.
When I have a towel from the linen of that flax,
Come and visit me, brothers, and see me wipe my tears.

The forest murmurs

The forest murmurs *kash-kash*, the forest murmurs.
Why does it keep on murmuring?
It wants every year to put on new branches.
The reeds murmur *kash-kash*, the reeds murmur.
Why do they keep on murmuring?
They want every year to increase their shoots.
The people buzz, the people buzz.
Why do they keep on buzzing?
They want every year to add new souls.

The eagle flies

The eagle flies in the blue under heaven,
   Ai, ai, in the blue under heaven.

And his nest is in the top of the oak tree.
   Ai, ai, in the top of the oak tree.

Our thoughts are within our whole life,
And our dreams through all its length,
   Ai, ai, through all its length.

We shall live until our legs fail under us,
And the light of our minds is spent,
   Ai, ai, until it is spent.

Boatmen's song

I

Verse
In time past when we were younger
And visited the mothers of our wives,
Our women folk carried pies,
And we carried barrels of beer.

Chorus
Yes, yes! ah yes!

Verse
When will it end, this life,
This boatman's misery?

Chorus
Yes, yes! ah yes!
Heave away! heave away!
Heave away! heave!

II

We are men from another place –
From the bazaar of Confusion,
From the village of Stupidity,
From the family of Folly.

Yes, yes! ah yes!

Will it soon be the end of this hardship,
Of the boatman's wandering life?

Heave away! heave!

III

Our wives are sitting at home
In shoes and white stockings,
While we toil here as boatmen
In our *lapti* and our *bakhils*.

Yes, yes! ah yes!

Oh, when will it end, this life,
This boatman's torment?

Heave away! Heave!

IV

By the river-bank fire
We freeze from night to morning,
But our wives are hoping
To see us home by Autumn.

Yes, yes! ah yes!

When will it end, this life,
This boatman's misery.

Heave away! heave!

V

At home our wives are hoping
We shall be bringing them money,
But toiling here as boatmen
We only gather fleas.

Yes, yes! ah yes!

Will it soon be the end of this hardship,
This boatman's life of wandering?

Heave away! heave!

(*lapti* – best sandals)
(*bakhils* – waders)

46

Barley I sowed

(Sung at the festival for the completion of autumn work in the fields)

Barley I sowed in the barley field
    Gently, gently.
The rain it fell with a *shibr-shibr* –
    Gently, gently.
After the rain the sun looked out
    Gently, gently.
Shoots of barley came out of the earth
    Gently, gently.
The barley ears grew fine and plump
    Gently, gently.
The barley grew plump, it was time to reap –
    Gently, gently.
The stalks grew up as firm as reeds –
    Gently, gently.
The grains grew fat, as fat as peas –
    Gently, gently.
I went to the field, along the edge
    Gently, gently.
I tried the barley and found it ripe –
    Gently, gently.
I reaped, I reaped, not hurrying,
    Gently, gently.
I finished reaping, decided to thresh
    Gently, gently.
I called my family together –
    Gently, gently.
With the family of the village we live –
    Gently, gently.
I prepared a hospitable feast –
    Gently, gently!
From three grains I made some malt
    Gently, gently.
On the palate of my mouth I steeped it
    Gently, gently.
On the crown of my head I dried it
    Gently, gently.
In a hand-mill I ground it –
    Gently, gently!

Beer I brewed and fermented it
  Gently, gently,
It runs away out of the barrel –
  Gently, gently!
I thought to invite seven villages –
  Gently, gently.
To feast three days with everyone –
  Gently, gently!
Now the guests have all assembled
  Gently, gently.
The little hut is filling up
  Gently, gently.
An elder with an old grey beard –
  Gently, gently! –
Breaks in pieces a great loaf –
  Gently, gently,
Observes the ritual, breaking it
  Gently, gently,
Gives it to all in turn to taste –
  Gently, gently.
The beer cup clinks in every hand –
  Gently, gently!
It makes strangers acquainted –
  Gently, gently.
The Chuvash people from of old –
  Gently, gently! –
After their labours meet and feast –
  Gently, gently.
Having drunk, they strike up songs –
  Gently, gently,
Dance without waiting to be asked –
  Gently, gently.
The women in the front corner –
  Gently, gently! –
Lend their voices to a new song –
  Gently, gently.
They start to sing *chastushkas* too –
  Gently, gently,
And hand the visiting presents around
  Gently, gently,
And one man blows into the *shabar*
  Gently, gently, –

48

Sweat runs in rivers down his face
　　Gently, gently.
They talk and make each other glad,
　　Gently, gently.
Then the cocks crow and the day breaks
　　Gently, gently!
And all go off to their own houses
　　Gently, gently.
So from age to age we live
　　Gently, gently.
We live on the earth and till the earth
　　Gently, gently,
And only in winter rest a little –
　　Gently, gently. . .

(*chastushka* – a popular song)

Out of the cellar

(guest song)

Out of the cellar flew the bright shining bird,
Sat on the table and preened itself.

See us on the way, good friends, it's time for us to go!

Out of the store cupboard flew the bright yellow bird,
Sat on the table and preened itself.

See us on the way, good friends!

Out of the store cupboard flew the bright yellow bird,
It pecks at your knees, it will peck you to death.

Hold on to your bird, good friends!

Out of the cellar flew the bright shining bird,
It pecks your head, it will peck you to death.

Hold on to it, good friends!

('bright shining bird' – home-distilled liquor)
('bright yellow bird' – Chuvash beer known as *sim-pyl*)

A lonely birch in the steppe

(table song)

There's a lonely birch in the steppe,
And on its top sits a white hawk;
Ai, ai, it sits on the birch,
But its wings are close to the sky.
Our comely bodies, like candles,
Stand here before our good elders,
And our thoughts are in our fathers' house.

Ai, ai, the hawk sits on the birch,
But its wings are close to the sky.
Our elders, sitting at table,
Your thoughts are close to your hearts;
But we who are foolish, our words
Tremble on the tips of our tongues.

Ai, ai, we have crossed twelve fields,
Walking from wheatfield to wheatfield.
The field's edge will not turn us from our way,
But treasures may turn us from the truth.
Let us not then look on the world's treasures –
Ruin may come upon our souls
Which are still so young and untried.

Guest songs

I

We shall not mow the grass without bending –
Let us do honour to the flowering grasses.
We shall not be feasted by our brothers without singing –
Let us do honour to the feast.

They told us to climb the high mountain,
To pluck there the leaves of the birch trees.
Our elders told us to sing to them,
To try out our unformed minds.

Dark lashes, ai, longer than eyes,
Long plaits, ai, lower than waists.
How shall we know strength of soul and mind?
By the words of the mouth, by its song.

Who would give me a silver ring,
I would give him my rings of gold.
The brother who would stand and sing with me,
I would give him one half of my soul.

A grey dove sits on the house roof,
But its shadow is out in the yard.
We who bow are here in your bright chamber,
But our voices are out in the village.

II

Have you come, our dear ones, have you come,
Will you not take off your sheepskin coats?
You have travelled long, on endless roads,
Did you want us to die in waiting?

In the steppe amidst the wild grasses
The birch tree stands green, alone –
Do not cut it down with a sharp axe,
Let it stand and adorn the steppe.

Within this house, dear friends,
Lives a man who is old;
Do not hurt him with rash words,
Let him live as the jewel of the house.

III

Shall we not harness the grey horse?
Not tie up its tail in a knot?
Not seat our host in his place?
Not put the cup in his hands?
Not bow and embrace his legs?
Not hear his words of greeting? –
Our heads are bowed before you,
Your words are sweet before us.

Dear friend, sit in your place, take the cup,
Let us remain bowing before you.
Which leg shall we embrace as we bow?
Will it be sweeter to your soul
If we bend and embrace your right leg?
Will your heart utter no reproach
If we embrace your left leg, bowing?

V

A little silver eye turns in the sun –
A silver ring with writing on it.
Ah, my slender waist and my young head
Turn in the dancing circle.

I have cut my hair like a Russian,
Every hair in a separate *nukhrat*.
The *nukhrat*'s light is like daylight,
We are mirrors of father and mother.

When I came to you, my dear ones,
I shone with joy like a buttercup,
Grew dark as a currant with shame,
Flushed red as a raspberry.

Leaving the village, I loosed my horse,
Fool that I am, forgetting the strawberries.
If I had remembered them,
I would have called back my horse.
I say at the table and joked,
Forgetting there were elders there.
Fool, if I had remembered,
I'd have bared my head and bowed low.

V

Brightly burns the broad taper,
If I let it go, I would not burn my hand.
I do not fear lest it burn my hand,
I fear lest it fall and go out.
And I do not fear the taper will go out,
I fear lest my dear ones grow cold to me.

There are ninety folds in my fur coat.
If these ninety folds come out,
It will lose its comely look.
If my dear ones grow cold and leave me,
My head will lose its honour.

Walk in peace lest the elders blame you.
Speak no insults, lest your dear ones grow cold.
Rather let fair days pass without profit
Than our dear ones be heavy of heart!
Rather let us gather up maple leaves
Than let sunny days pass without profit.
Maple leaves cannot become paper,
Our dear ones cannot become strangers.

And snow will not fall, if we do not sing.
And night will not come, if we do not talk.
But snow will fall and night come, brother,
And what can compare with this life
Lived in harmony with our dear ones?

VI

Oh the blue flower, deep in the forest!
Its crown breaks open, and its sound
Completes the forest's fullness.
Oh father and mother of ours,
We come before you and greet you,
Completing the fullness of our house.

Oh mother, you are a skein of silk!
A skein of silken threads!
When we come, you unwind yourself,
And then when we go on our way,
You wind yourself up again.

VII

The wind already whirls, ai-ai, it whirls,
Branches of wild cherry wrap round the willow.
If you do not think, it is not so bitter,
When you think, you can hardly stand up.

Oh to count the stars in the sky!
How many should we count for just one to be moved?
Do not our belts fall from our waists?
Does our life not pass us by?

Ah, the cloud floats and floats,
Like the round cap I wear on my head.
Ah, time passes, life passes,
Like a dream that we see without sleep.

(*nukhrat* – a Bulgarian coin)

Ah, the game
(song for choral dance)

Ah, the game, the circling game!
And the top of the circling game
Is the top of the spreading elm;
The top of the elm is swaying,
Dropping us into fire and water.
Between the fire and the water
I have brewed a beer like fire,
I have gathered the guests like hair,
I have made them play like dolls,
And then scattered them like chickens:

– In your rows, in your rows – *kysh!* –
And off you go!

I went out into the field

(song for the evening gatherings known as *ullakh*)

I went out into the field –
Not one haycock did I see.
I came into the village –
And not one girl did I see.
Where were they then, oh where?
In the white hut in the village
They had gathered and were sitting
And knotting the open lace.

I looked in the window and I saw
They were betrothing my beloved.
In a white dress they had decked her,
Placed a beaker in her hands
And she stood before the table.

Out in the street I wept,
Rocking outside the window.
Let him who takes my love
Lie bedridden for nine years,
Lie sick, not able to rise,
And go six years without walking.

Little straw

(Sung for the festival of the 'Maidens' Beer')

Little straw, little straw, beauty of the earth!
The straw will be blown by the wind,
And a joke will be the end
Of the beauty of the earth!

A fox-fur cap is the beauty of the head,
And this girl's beer is the beauty of this house;
When this girl's beer
Is all drunk up,
A joke will be the end
Of the beauty of this house.

Oh elders, we bow down to you
Who have come to visit us!
You will go forth, dear ones,
But your beauty will not end.
And we shall not depart
From our ancient ways,
Nor bring in new ways.

Speech of the best man at a wedding
(shortened version)

Salaam-alec, good health to you!

Are you drinking, eating, playing, laughing,
are you happy to receive us?
If you are, take three steps forward,
if not, take three steps back.
Old ones and young ones, will you receive us?

(*All*: Gladly we receive you!)

To the bride's house we rode
between earth and heaven.
As we rode between earth and heaven,
we espied a tree.
Look from afar – it is black,
come closer – it seems white.
We looked up, and saw a nest.
We climbed up and looked –
and could not tell what nest it was.
Whose then was that nest?

(*All*: The nest of the bridegroom and bride.)

Riding fifty miles over open fields,
We came upon a bed of reeds.
In the reeds we saw a marvel:
look from one side – they are happy,
from the other – they are sad.
And this is what they're saying:
'They are always taking from me,
and yet I grow and grow'.
What sort of thing is this?

(*All*: The bridegroom and the bride.)

When we had ridden fifty miles,
we came to the bride's father's village.
The village seemed like a town,
the bride's father's house like a palace.

In the bride's father's courtyard
stands a house that measures twelve *sazhens*
made of six score logs.
Next to it is a porch
made of eighteen planks,
and three steps lead up to it.
On one of the steps you stand,
on another we stand,
and on the third stands my horse.
We have no leave to enter.
If it please you, we shall enter,
if not, we shall not enter.

(*All:* Please come in! *They go in.*)

This bride's father's house is spacious,
from the courtyard you see six corners,
from inside you see four corners.
The floor is of ninety-nine boards.
Of all those ninety-nine
is there not one that is free
for our play and our rejoicing?
It is not we who ask,
but our bridegroom asks.
In the bride's father's house, we see,
there are eighty-eight beds,
on one of the eighty-eight
shall we not be given leave
to sit down and rest?
And not only we
but the high-soaring eagle
sits to rest on the juniper . . .

(*All:* Please sit down. *They sit.*)

The bride's father has made beer
of seven *poods* of grain stored twelve years,
he has dried the malt on glass
and ground it with a round stone.
The bride's father, we see,
has a cellar three *sazhens* deep
and a forty-pail barrel

60

with two bungs and forty hoops.
Open one bung,
and sweet sherbet flows out,
open the other,
and out flows *sim-pyl*.
Drink *sim-pyl*, you will be drunk,
drink sweet sherbet,
you will speak sweetly,
you will laugh and play.
And in talk sweet as sherbet,
playing and laughing,
let us pass this wedding, sweet friends.

(*All:* Peace and blessing to you. *The festivities begin.*)

(*sazhen* – measure of length, about 7 feet)
(*sim-pyl* – home-brewed beer)

We have come for the wedding
(sung by those taking part in the bride's wedding procession)

We have come, we have come for the wedding,
One hundred and one we have come,
Shaking the earth as we came.
One hundred and one we came here,
Just one hundred we shall go hence.

We have brought a girl like a sheaf of corn,
Do not change her into chaff.

We have brought a girl with rosy cheeks,
Do not change them into white linen.

The bride, like a silk kerchief,
We have given to the son-in-law.
Before we return again,
Do not change this silk to linen,
Do not tear her and crumple her.

The bride, like the juice of berries,
We have given to the mother-in-law.
Before we return again,
Do not change her to river water,
Do not spill her and scatter her.

Song of the bride's friends

Our brother-in-law is as handsome
As a twisted birch-tree stump,
His head like a sick sheep's head,
His mouth like a yeast bowl's mouth.

Take off the hat from his head:
He's like a mushroom in dung.
Marry! he'd be better to sit
In the granary sifting the chaff.

In our fields are long ears of barley,
Bent so low they can't stand upright;
And he can't open his eyes,
His lashes have grown so long!

Oh brother-in-law, poor brother,
Out of three *poods* of bast,
He can barely make one slipper,
And that one turns out crooked.
It's not so bad that it's crooked,
It was bought at the market as well!

Other brothers-in-law are like silk,
You tuck them away, they slip out;
But ours is just a bear,
You meet him, he bites your head off!

No, we won't give our sister away!
But when we come closer, we'll see.
If seven times five heads bow to us,
Well, then we may think again!

Will the bride come out to us?
(Wedding song, sung by the whole company)

Will the bride come out to us, or won't she?
Now we are going off home.
When dawn whitened we made her
White-headed under her veil.

Now red day has begun
Is it not time for us all
To see our bride
With a red face now?

If she is quickly ready,
She will be in her own adornment,
But if she is not ready quickly,
Her adornment will not be hers.

Our father's horse, his brown horse,
Stamps his hooves impatiently –
You must answer its call
And come out to please our father.

And henceforth, to please our mother,
Get up when the cow lows at dawn,
But to please our brother-in-law,
Do not rise before the sun.

We await from you a dowry
To make the cart give way.
We have thrown in enough silver
To make the tables buckle.

Ah, the old ones in this house
Will have rest for their feet –
A light-footed one has come,
To put a cushion under their feet.

Bride's lament

Oh, our elders, forgive me!
Allow me my tears!
Old grandfather Yaruk,
You have a house with buildings,
Like half of a forest,
But your kindness is still greater,
Allow me my weeping!

*

Oh father, oh mother!
In seven summer months,
And in seventy different days
There will be one day of storms
It will trample and scatter the grain
Which has only just ripened.
The folk with a big family
Will collect it with their family,
But who will help you gather it?
Not remembering me till then,
Perhaps then you will remember me.

*

Bel-bel the flower, bel the flower,
Its petals shaking over the hive –
They seem on the point of falling.
Ere I cross my father's threshold,
May my soul not go from me.

*

By the highway grow wild grasses,
And the tops of the grass are pearls.
But who will gather these pearls?
He who walks the road will gather them.
By the highway grow the birch trees,
The birch leaves covered with letters,
The leaves of the birch are writing.
But who will read those letters?

65

He who wrote them, he will read them.
But who knows my fate?
He who gave it to me, he knows it.

*

Oh, father, father,
When I rocked the cradle,
When I stood on two feet
And began to walk before you,
You taught me sense and reason –
How then in the future
Will you manage to do this?

*

Oh, mother, mother,
You will scour the linen,
With ash to your elbows;
You will rinse the linen,
Splashing water to your waist.
Oh, mother, mother,
You will wash the linen
And come running home,
You will search the hut, mother,
But there's no daughter to help you,
She is gone beyond call.

*

Oh, my friends, my sweet girls,
Whose souls lay close to mine,
From you I have been parted
As flax from hemp is parted!
Oh, dear elders of our people,
Oh, my village, my own family,
May my name remain with you!
What remains of a good horse?
He has travelled many roads –
Only that remains of him.
What will now remain of me?
All the good I have seen was with you –
Only that will remain.

Parents' valediction to the bride and bridegroom

Oh our son, yellow gold!
Oh our daughter, white gold!

Not we brought into the world
The custom of marriage,
Nor did we receive it
From foreign lands.

And the birds, joined in marriage,
Bring us their young ones;
And the bees, in peaceful marriage,
Store up their honey.
And now you, our children,
Joining in marriage,
Stand here before us.

You made us glad until the time
When we grew grey, then grew white –
In our cares and our consolations
You made our hair go white,
Just so may yours go white.

You knelt to us lovingly,
Lovingly you bow to us –
In the same way may others
Respect you and bow to you.

Live joyfully as orioles,
Fluttering with emotion together
As eagles' wings flutter;
As swans, in loving harmony,
Joyfully fluff up their soft down –
Just so be soft to one another,
Fluffing the soft down of love.

Joining together, as eagles join,
You will lie down two
And will rise up three.

Be generous as the field,
Be rich as the forest.
Abound like the nut-wood
In shoots and sprouts.

Know the business of day
And the business of night,
Understand them with one mind –
On that, life is founded.

Let your wife be with child
As many times as may be.
We would wish for her
A fruitful womb
Twelve times over.
May she bear nine sons
And three daughters.

Let your daughters be fitting
For other houses and families;
And let your sons be pleasing
To our village society
And to our neighbours.

And may you multiply
From generation to generation.
May the son's foot tread
Where the father's foot has trodden.
May the daughter-in-law follow
In the mother-in-law's footsteps.

May your table be hospitable
With bread and with salt;
May the good spirit Thrift
Not leave your granary
Or desert your larder.

May your bed be spacious
For children's merriment,
May your yard be spacious
For cattle and all beasts.

Fear God – the most high Tura,
Be chaste and modest
Before the sons and daughters
Of the race of men.

Respect our elders,
Do not disobey them.

Do not take into the village
The words of your house;
Nor take into your house
The words of the street.
Be fitting for the people
Of our village, our one family.
Do not be higher than the word
Of your father and your mother.

May the man not seek refuge
Behind the wife's back;
May the woman not possess
Power over her husband.
May she be the warmth of the house.

Let her be welcoming
To every guest and stranger.

When she goes to fetch water,
May she not stay for the laggard,
But may she overtake
The one who goes ahead.

Remember that the wealth of the house is love.

Be as wise as our grandfathers
And their fathers before them.

With the old be as old people,
With the young be young.

Live till you are old and weak,
Till your mind is feeble,
Till you wind your foot-wrappings

Around your heads,
And the *surban* from your heads
Around your feet.

Oh you our elders!
Grandfathers and ancestors!
Thanks to you, dear elders,
That you have deigned to come
And bring us your good wishes,
And we beg of you to watch
And make sure that what is right
Is performed by us
Without error or fault.

Oh Tura!
Look kindly
On our young Word.
We have said too much, we know,
Forgive us our foolishness,
For we do not know all things.

Now one last word to you,
Our son, yellow gold,
And our daughter, white gold.
You are going from us.
Go into the world and its people.
You are free to go forth!
We make you free.

Our wedding party!
Village neighbours – great family!
We beg you: eat and drink,
Sing and dance!
Be merry with us!

Peace be with you and blessing!
May the light of Happiness
Descend on your heads.

Conscript songs

I

Alas, our souls are here on earth
For the sorrow of this world;
The seeds of the world's sorrow
Are in our young heads.

We were comely as white candles,
With eyes that seemed given by heaven.
When they light the top of a candle,
This head of fire burns
Melting all the candle's body.
And with sorrow our heads are burning,
Consuming us utterly.

II

On both sides of the road
On which we must depart
Flax flowers – blue petals – are scattered.

On both sides of the road
On which we shall depart
Are white cups of white flowers.

On both sides of the road
On which we are departing
To the world's edge stand iron barriers
And at the edge of the world
The eye of a needle.

III

On the bank of the broad river stands a copper pole,
And on the pole is a yellow candle;
High burns the candle, deep it is reflected –
The eyes of the red fox will not see it.
Our souls burn before our loved ones,
And they will not see the flame.

Our mother was a she-eagle,
She sent us out in the morning,
Gathered us together in the evening.
Whom now in the evenings
Will you gather together, mother?

IV

There are seven of us, boys of an age,
Build high seven fences, friends –
Fence us in and let us stay here.

We have seven girls for sweethearts,
Drape us with seven white cloths,
Drape us, dear friends, and save us.

My mother's stove is a white one –
Shall I look at it before going,
Or go on my way with closed eyes?

In my father's house the floors are painted –
Shall I walk right across them,
Or crawl over them before going?

72

Amidst the plain

Amidst the plain is a spreading oak,
I went up, thinking it was my father,
But it didn't call out: Approach, my son –

I grew sad, and I began to weep.

Amidst the field is a branching linden,
I went up, thinking it was my mother,
But it didn't say: Approach, little son –

I grew lonely, and I began to weep.

Amidst the valley is a lonely willow,
I went up, thinking it was my beloved,
But it didn't murmur: Approach, my love –

My heart ached, and I began to sob.

Soldiers' song

Through the star we see a road –
Is it not the one we must go away on?

Through the moon we see a plain –
Is it not the one we must go away on?

Through the sun we see a girl –
Is she not the one we must leave behind?

Through the oak we see blood –
Is that not our blood that we see?

Across the road we see a field –
Is it not the one where we shall remain?

Murder in the forest

A-ah, Idabay, Idabay!
I said: let us stay the night here.
No, you would not stay the night,
You went, for you sensed disaster.

Sorrowful the elm in the forest,
Oh, how its twigs all tremble! . . .

Get up, Idabay, get up –
Tonight they will murder us –
Shadows loom under the oak,
Dear Kaverle and Sakhar!

Like a good horse's collar
Is the silver upon my breast –
Tonight they will murder us –
Let my silver become
A ring around the moon!
Dear Kaverle and Sakhar!
My house is full of young folk –
Tonight they will murder us –
May they fly away like angels!
Dear Kaverle and Sakhar!
I am wearing my linen kaftan –
Tonight they will murder us –
May it turn to a cloud and float off!
Dear Kaverle and Sakhar!
As broad as the palm of my hand
Is my embroidered *masmak* –
Tonight they will murder us –
May it turn into a rainbow!
Dear Kaverle and Sakhar!

(*masmak* – a ribbon)

Dead man's song

(performed in the name of the deceased by a relative)

At the time when the berries
Of the earth were ripening,
I parted from earth and its waters.
At the time when the crops were ripening,
I parted from the people of my clan.
My time was all used up,
I was taken away from the table.
The sash from around my waist
I leave hanging on its hook.
My chair has been taken from the table,
Turn it upside down!
Give my food to the dog,
But don't give it to the cat!

And you, and you!
Will you come with me?
If you come, better straight away.
Will you come, will you come with me?
If you come, then come straight away!

Funeral song

The cuckoo flies in with its voice,
With your voice you'll not come again!
The nightingale flies in with its song,
With your song you'll not come again!
The swallow flies in with its chatter,
With your chatter you'll not come again!
The dawn breaks in whiteness,
In whiteness you'll not come again!
The sun rises in redness,
Never again will you walk in redness!
The waters flow by with their murmur,
With a murmur you'll not come again!

Song of the hare

On a high hill the strong wind
Has made my ears ring,
Dancing cold on the ice,
My legs have gone numb.

Gnawing at the frozen oak,
My lips have begun to crack.
Here they come, by twos, by threes –
I can see them coming to hunt me.

They will catch me and tear off my skin,
And go to the market and sell it,
They will sell my skin and get drunk,
And then they will go back home.

They will get drunk, and go back home,
And then they will beat their wives,
They will give their wives a thrashing,
And the children will cry.

And the children will cry,
Oh, how sad! how sad!
The children will cry,
How sad! how sad!

Our father is the sazan fish

Our father is the sazan fish –
From lake to lake he plunges,
Never gives guests soup without fish.

Our mother is the mother bee –
From flower to flower she flits,
Never gives guests beer without honey.

Our elder brother is the storm –
He never sends rain without wind,
Ay-ara, yay-a, yai-yai-yur!

Our daughter-in-law is millet porridge –
In the house she stirs up the whole family,
Ay-ara, yay-a, yai-yai-yur!

But our little sister is the flighty one –
All day from bazaar to bazaar,
Till the bottom of the purse is empty –

Ay-ara, yay-a yai-yai-yur!

Cradle songs

To our darling baby
We shall give baby legs,
To go hop, hop, hop,
To go gallop-a-gallop,
To mother a comb,
To baby little wings,
To fly so high,
Guli-guli fly high.

Bumble-bee hill, Bumble-bee hill!
On Bumble-bee hill is the bumble-bee's nest,
In the bumble-bee's nest there are honeycombs,
In the honeycombs there is honey.
This little rogue
For his mother and father
Is gold and silver;
But for strangers no doubt
He is not even rubbish
On a shovel in the yard.

Chu-chu, chuchune!

The bark of the elm is the cradle,
The stem of the cherry the hoop,
The rowan the pole for rocking,
The hawthorn a hook for the cradle,
And the lime tree gives bast to make cord.
Linen of five strands – the wrappings,
Linen of six strands – a sheet,
Linen of seven strands – a blanket,
Linen of eight strands – a rug,
Linen of nine strands – a pillow,
Linen of ten strands – a quilt,
Linen of eleven strands – some trousers,
Linen of twelve strands – a shirt,
Linen of thirteen strands – an apron,

Linen of fourteen strands – a scarf,
Linen of fifteen strands – a cap,

Chu-chu, chuchune!

To buy such a one no treasure would serve,
Fear of losing him would rob me of my soul!
Mother and father gave him birth,
Wrapped him in white swaddling clothes,
Laid him over the warm stove,
Smeared his little mouth with honey,
Wished our darling happiness,

Chu-chu, chuchune!

These are his hands,
And these are his feet,
And we take them and play with them,
Nya-nya,
Pa-pa,
Ee-ee-ee . . .

III

Chuchi-chuchi Chulandai!
Papki-papki Palandai!

Father has gone to market,
Mother has gone to pick berries,
She picked, she picked, she was sleepy,
Lay down on the grass and slept . . .
And the lightning flashed,
And the thunder roared,
And the rain wet her through . . .
And the soup is not tasty,
The shirts are not washed –
Let the thunder crash,
Let the lightning flash –
Let them wake mother up.

81

First steps
(rhymes for teaching children to walk)

I

The bear has lost his leg,
And our little one has got it.
The wolf has lost his leg,
It is on our little one.

II

The cat's leg it is jelly,
Our Illembi's leg is iron.
The dog's leg it is rotten,
Our Illembi's leg is alive.

Bath songs for children

(sung when the child is being beaten with birch twigs
in the steam bath)

Forty-one birch leaves!
Let our Senti sweat
Forty-one drops of sweat!
Let it make him strong and healthy!
Let bitterness go and sweetness remain,
Let the black go away and the precious remain!
Grow quickly like hops,
Grow broadly like leaves!
Kash-kash-kashmanan,
Our Senti is an ataman.
By evening you'll grow to the ceiling,
By morning you'll be like a pole!
Let your good head incline to goodness,
Let your good feet walk in goodness
With the step of goodness!
May your good hands
Do good deeds!

Sun, come here!

(children's song)

Sun, little sun, come here!
Come along, come along!
Your baby has fallen in the river,
Pull him out
With your golden poker!
To him I will give a red egg
And a white one to you!

Chi-chi, tom tit

(children's song)

Chi-chi, tom tit,
Where are you going to, tom tit?
– To steal a bit of hemp seed.
– What if the farmer sees?
– I'll fly and hide in the pine tree.
– And what if you go hungry?
– I'll peck at the pine cones.
– What if they stick in your gullet?
– I'll poke and I'll pull them out.
– And what if you start bleeding?
– I'll dip in the water and wash.
– And what if your wings are frozen?
– I'll light a fire for warmth.
– And what if the fire starts spreading?
– I'll stamp and I'll put it out.
– And what if you break your leg then?
– I'll find a smith to mend it.
– And what if you can't find one?
– I'll find a tinker to mend it.
– And what if you can't find one?
– I'll go and find Alatyr.
– And what if you can't find him?
– I'll go to Simbirsk to get mended.
– And what if you can't find Simbirsk?
– Then I'll stamp and I'll stamp and I'll throw myself
Straight into the trap!

III

*Poems and Ethnographic Writing
of the Modern Period*

Chavash Khveti

(Khvedyá Chuvash)

(died after 1834)

The first Chuvash poet whose name is known. An illiterate peasant. His poems were recorded from his performance by the Russian poet D.P. Oznobishiny. A.A. Fuks, a woman poet from Kazan who was Pushkin's friend, helped in their publication.

On the fir tree sings the cuckoo

On the fir tree sings the cuckoo;
In the rye the corncrake sings;
The nightingale sings in the cherry;
And should we too not want to sing?
Black Vaska has happiness;
And the rich man has sorrow enough:
One rouble is not a hundred roubles,
A hundred roubles not a thousand.

And the carefree girls went out
Picking flowers in the yellow field,
And down came the yellow rain,
And they found only yellow hawksbeard.
If it is not touched by maiden's hands,
The hollow hawksbeard will not burst;
If they are not touched by the boys' hands,
The maiden's breasts will never grow.
Come then, girls to the *posidelki*,
I have hazel nuts for you
The size of a mouse's nut;
I shall crack the nuts for you,
And you shall have them as a treat.

(*posidelki* – evening gatherings of village people)

Bay, bay, bay horse

Bay, bay, bay horse!
You are tired with galloping to the wedding.
Bay, bay, little bay!
We say, not being acquainted
With the manners of the towns:
Bride of ours, how fine you are,
And how finely you are dressed!
As if on a thousand sleighs
We have galloped to bring you home.
Guests, stamp, and stamp the floor,
Stamp the floor and dance and leap!
Be merry, and laugh your fill!
Our father's horse, his blue-grey horse,
Slipped on the blue ice and stayed there;
Our father's horse, his black horse,
Slipped in the black mud and stayed there;
Our father's horse, his brown horse,
Slipped in the black mud and stayed there;
Our father's horse, his brown horse,
Our brother-in-law rode him into the ground.
Hops of the meadow, hops of the meadow,
Every hop as big as an apple!
It was the hops played tricks on me:
My legs are going in all directions.
Hops of the garden, hops of the garden,
Every hop is like a dumpling!
I tried one, taking it for a dumpling,
And it played wicked tricks on me:
It took me by my brown hair
And pulled me down to the ground.
There is no use in a drunken man;
There is no soul in a dead man;
There is no light in a quenched taper;
From the dark expect nothing but dark,
Light is found only in the light!
Soft the pillow, soft the quilt –
Do not go to sleep and rest on them,
But when there is a fire burning,
How can the fire not bring you rest? . . .
I jumbled it, mixed it all up;

Mixed up the autumn and the spring,
I went outside and I ran,
In the bath house I broke the stove,
And my father heard it and caught me,
And beat me with an elm-wood stick.

So I have sung my song,
May my song remain in the village,
And my hands remain on my girl.

Maksam Fyodorov

(Maksim Fyodorov)

(died after 1852)

Worked as a clerk in one of the local district councils in the Kurmysh district of the Simbirsk region, then from 1838 in a government office in the town of Alatyr. His poem 'We are the Chuvash', printed in 1852 in Russian transcription in a Petersburg journal, remained for a long time anonymous. The findings of the Chuvash historian V.D. Dimitriev, published in 1981, establish that Fyodorov was indeed the author.

We are the Chuvash people

We are the Chuvash people.
We travelled to the Atal
And densely we settled there.
Now the clerks are all asking:
Where do the Chuvash come from?
We Chuvash are Chuvash,
Our kindred are the Tatars,
And our language is Chuvash.
When misfortune happens,
We turn to Tura,
And to the Kiremet
We sacrifice cows and calves;
May God send us health,
May he send us happiness.
We cannot make writing,
We don't know how to count;
We ask our little father:
What we should do in misfortune?
What should we give to the clerks?
And that is how we live,
And find our happiness;
We pass the time in smoking;
What of it? It brings happiness!
Animals too we keep:
Horses, pigs, birds and cows;
We have milk, eggs and honey;

Eat your black bread, Chuvash people,
And sell your cattle,
And then you'll have silver
To keep the clerks from misery.
Eat your black bread, Chuvash people.
What of it? It brings happiness!

(*Atal* – The Volga river)
(*Kiremet* – spirit of the dead)

91

Sepritun Yantush

(Sepridun Yandush)

(1821–1861)

The first Chuvash writer, ethnographer and historian, Sepridun Yandush (Spiridon Mikhailovich Mikhailov) was born in the town of Yungabus in the Murgash district. At the age of ten he was handed over by his parents to a merchant of their acquaintance, to be a domestic servant in the town of Kozmodemyansk. Learning to read and write on his own initiative, he became assistant clerk in a government office. Ten years later he was appointed as translator in this office, and worked in this capacity for the rest of his life.

From the year 1852 he began to publish stories, sketches and ethnographic studies about the Russians, the Chuvash and the Cheremisses. In 1852 appeared his book 'On Chuvash Music' followed by 'Chuvash Tales and Stories' (1853) and 'Popular Customs of the Kozmodemyansk Region' (1855). He was elected a fellow of the Russian Geographical Society in 1854 and awarded the silver medal of the Society in 1859.

In the absence of a Chuvash alphabet, he wrote in Russian.

Bride's Lament

When the dances are finished, the bride is led into a hut under a veil; there a feather mattress is laid out for her behind a curtain and a table is spread with food, usually the cakes known as *syugyu* and the pancakes known as *chigyt*, and with beer and wine. Coming in from the right-hand end of the table, the bride takes her seat on the feather mattress (*tyuzhek*), drawing back a little the curtain (*chadyr*). A married sister or some other female relative sits down beside her and teaches her how to *wail*, wailing three times herself (and bride's lament is literally called a *wail* in Chuvash). The bride wails tearfully and repeats these words: 'Oh father! oh mother! you haven't loved me, you have deserted me, you are giving me away; my work cannot have pleased you.' Turning to her brothers and sisters, she wails: 'Oh darling brother, to you I speak! Oh darling sister, to you I speak!' She uses a great many words in her wailing. If someone who knows the Chuvash language is near to the weeping bride at this time, he will find her expressions very moving, particularly when she

92

begins to bewail her native fields, woods and waters, the cradle of her childhood, her upbringing by her parents, their good actions, their labours, and the bitterness of parting with her native place and its people, her future fate among the descendants of another tribal ancestor, and in this case her lament resembles the following verses:

> Oh you, Yunga, place of my birth,
> Where the cradle received me,
> I shed tears as I bid you farewell!
> A sad orphan I have become.
>
> Farewell, land of my fathers,
> Farewell, days of my youth!
> I shall not stop loving you,
> When I go off to foreign places.
>
> My horse has not carried me all away:
> Here I leave a part of my life,
> Take it, take it for ever,
> I make you a gift of my heart!

In this manner the bride, continuing to wail, embraces in turn all those who come up to her, beginning with her parents and other relations, then all the peasants from her village, the women, the girls and even the little children, finding suitable words for each one and weeping disconsolately at the top of her voice. At the same time, she presents each ot them with a mug of beer, into which they place a small coin for her, from half a copeck to fifty copecks, depending on their wealth. This money is called the *khyukh uksi*, the 'wailing money', or rather the 'tribute of the lament', and the bride puts it away, either in a pocket, or on the mattress where she is sitting. This ceremony lasts for several hours, until the bride is taken away by the groom. To speak from my own experience, I was once at a Chuvash wedding, sitting beside the bride, when she embraced me and started wailing: 'Oh, dear brother of mine! Let me shed bitter tears for you; forgive me, don't be offended, forgive me now, *piren yra ulbut* (our good master) and do not forget my heartfelt tears.' At these touching words I could not stop myself bursting into tears, perhaps because this wailing woman was my own sister Tatyana . . .

(from the book 'Chuvash Weddings' (1852), written in Russian)

93

Vasily Magnitsky

(Vasily Magnitsky)

(1839–1901)

Russian by birth, but with an excellent knowledge of Chuvash, Vasily Konstantinovich Magnitsky devoted his life to the study of Chuvash history, religion and popular oral literature. His 'Contributions to an Explanation of the Old Chuvash Faith' (Kazan, 1881) still retains its scholarly and artistic value. He was born in the village of Yedrne in the family of a priest, studied at a religious seminary and the law faculty of Kazan University, and worked as a police investigator and then, from 1887 until his death, as inspector of schools in the Vyatsk and Kazan regions.

The stealing of the earth

If, in spite of exact observation of the Field and Rain Sacrifices, there is a succession of bad harvests in some place, the Chuvash people of that place set off at night in a wedding procession to fertile places, in order to steal the earth itself.

Noticing over several years the gradual decline of the grain harvest, the elders gather in one of the big bazaars and there, in some place apart from the people of other villages, they begin to hold forth, among other things about the bad harvest. After long discussions, the old inhabitants, who are knowledgeable about the way to put things right, hint that a good harvest could be transferred to their fields from a distant place by certain methods known to them. Without much further consideration a unanimous decision is taken to undertake this task *for the general good*. It is done in the following manner.

First comes the preparation for the journey to foreign fields *in search of earth*: malt is collected from the villages for brewing beer. But the chief business here is not the beer and food for those who are going off in search of earth, but the choice of an honest young man to play the chief role, that of *bridegroom*, who will on certain conditions go to the chosen place to woo the *earth-bride*; without him success is impossible. The fate of this bridegroom is a terrible one,

94

according to Chuvash belief. However strong he may be in body, however favourable the circumstances of his subsequent life, he will not reach old age, but is certain to die before his time. Even so, fearful as this future may be, men can still be found who are eager to play the bridegroom. They are generally poor, homeless orphans, for whom the present is no more cheerful than a terrible future. When such a bridegroom has been found, he is invited to a general meeting held in the house of one of the old inhabitants of the village, he is given beer to drink, proper bridegroom's clothes are made for him, he is given what he needs for the future as far as is possible, and a time is appointed for going to bring home the earth-bride. On the day of departure, there is further eating and drinking, and at nightfall the procession, consisting of several carts and people with songs and music (played on the *shabar*) sets out on the road to the earth-bride. When the people cross the boundaries of their district, the songs and music are hushed, and even the little bells on the shaft-bows are tied up lest the people should be detected and caught and consequently thrashed to within an inch of their lives. Quietly approaching a field that is sown with corn, the procession stops, and the bridegroom of the earth is lifted down from the first cart by his fellows. Then they all equip themselves to collect the earth-bride. The oldest man present, playing the part of the bridegroom's father, stands next to him, facing the field of corn, and begins to speak:

'We have come to you here with a handsome clever bridegroom, oh rich and beloved earth-bride; we know that your wealth cannot be counted, but the ardour of our bridegroom's love cannot be told.'

The bridegroom bows down to the earth. The old man continues: 'So love our bridegroom too, dear bride, and do not refuse our request.'

The bridegroom bows again.

'Bring with you, dear bride, all your dowry, from fields and from meadows, from forests and from rivers.'

There is another prolonged bow, during which the people carry earth with shovels and spades into their carts. Then they lift up the groom, seat him in the first cart and race off at full speed for their own fields. Once they have reached their territory, they untie the bells, and again there are merry songs, music, shouting and the clapping of hands.

Approaching the chosen place, the bridegroom, who is now married, gets down from the cart by himself, and taking a spade, he goes up to his own cart and then to the others with these words:

'Welcome, dear new wife, I love you more than gold, more than my life; in return for my love, spread your dowry over our fields and meadows and forests and rivers.'

Then he takes a spadeful of earth from every cart and scatters it on the field; the remaining earth is scattered by his companions on the subsequent journey to the place where they live. The rest of this wedding night is spent in feasting, but on the following day and thereafter there are no further meetings.

(from 'Contributions to an Explanation of the Old Chuvash Faith', written in Russian)

96

Mikhail Fyodorov

(Mikhail Fyodorov)

(1848–1904)

Born in the village of Khurapkha in the Sundyr district, in a poor peasant family. Attended the Samara teachers' training college and – as an external student – the teachers' training course at the Kazan Teaching Institute. Taught in Cheboksary from 1879 to 1891, after which he was an inspector of schools.

His classic ballad 'Arzyuri', based on a careful study of Chuvash folklore, was written in 1879. For many years it circulated in manuscript, and was only published in 1908 in I.Y. Yakovlev's anthology 'Stories and Legends of the Chuvash'.

Arzyuri the wood demon
(extract from the ballad)

When the stay-at-home comes out
There will be a storm.
(folk saying)

. . . The Eastern sky grows red,
The fine weather is breaking,
Black clouds are racing.
From the graveyard they rise up
And vanish into nothing!
The black wood is raging,
The black horse snorts.
– Don't snort, black horse,
Why fear the elm tree?
And look at him, good friends,
He jogs along somehow;
Feed him with rye straw
And the good horse soon grows tired.
The rascal, he's not pulling,
Hardly moving his legs.
The road is bad in spring;
On our left hand there's a bump,
On our right a deep hollow,
On all sides pits and ruts,

97

Where can we find a flat place?
It's pitch dark, you can't see,
Can't make out what's over there –
Mile-post, devil or wood demon,
Or some spirit or a robber.
The soul quakes, the heart trembles,
From the crown of the head come fumes.
Like a man it whistles 'shevyk',
Something mutters and grumbles,
Something crushes and crashes –
The wood demon at his tricks,
Telling stories, talking nonsense,
Leading poor folk astray,
Mixing up all the distances.
Look, now you can see him:
Whirling like a whirlwind,
Breaking branches of bird cherry,
He leaps up from the hollow,
Breaks the shaft bow in two pieces.
Like an old white-bearded man
With the horns of a goat,
Pop-eyed and long-legged,
He races up and down
In the Urkhas-Kushak wood.
Like a mad dog he rages,
Puffs, spits and pushes you
Or tickles you to death.
Or he harnesses the horse,
And transformed into a Tatar,
He shakes the earth galloping,
Makes earth tremble with his shouts.
God have mercy, don't leave us,
Defend your creation!
God Pikhambar, our protector,
Call your dog to order.
Must we die here on this road?
Better die when you reach home,
Better die a proper death,
Live till senile old age
And die in your own bed.
If I died a peaceful death,
They would say: 'He was no kitten',

And quietly, not hurrying,
Setting all things in order,
Would give me an ancient burial.
The rich man dies, his wealth remains,
The good man dies, his name remains,
If I die now, what will remain?
My wife, my dark-skinned wife
Will remain behind to grieve.
My little foolish children
Have never yet held a plough.
Who will look after my son?
Who have pity on my daughter?
Better than be an orphan
To become a dead branch
Blown off by the autumn wind,
Blown away over the field
And vanish in the mill pond . . .

Ivan Yakovlev

(Ivan Yakovlev)

(1848–1930)

The Chuvash people regard Yakovlev as the patriarch of their culture. His life and work are described in the Introduction, pp. xxi-xxiii.

To the Chuvash intelligentsia

(extract from his spiritual testament)

I am speaking to the Chuvash who have had the good fortune to find light in education. Remember! You must help those who have not known this blessing; you must not expect others to help them. Never rely on outsiders! You came from this people, and it is your duty to enlighten the rest, to bring them light, illumination. Gathering up the treasure that education has given you, give it back to your people, explain to them and teach them what a true citizen of our native land must be like; teach them the law and the truth that must reside in the people. This is your duty, your obligation, since you have come from this people.

Do not be ashamed of the poverty and ignorance of your own people; you are one flesh and blood with them, and you must labour on their behalf. Only then will you return the debt you owe for the wisdom you have gathered from the strength and intelligence of the people. If you do not forget your debt to your younger brethren, the people will always repay you a hundred-fold. Do not forget this; bear it always in mind! . . .

Be friendly one to another, be modest. Keep clear of quarrels and backbiting. Let the great word of our Saviour be with you, who said: 'Love your enemies'. Unworthy deeds are often done among us, I have often seen it happen. Do not stand in the way of those who are going forward, do not molest them, for if you do so, you will destroy the good hopes of the foremost, and will be left with nothing. Help those who are going forward to reach

100

the heights, and may those who are climbing strongly give you their hands and help you to climb with them. If the front wheel advances, the back wheel will not lag behind. Live, listen attentively to one another, do good to one another. In this way you will endow existence with a power for life. Live and remember this always!

(1921)

Nikifor Okhotnikov

(Nikifor Okhotnikov)

(1860–1892)

Born in the village of Chuvash Shubarshkara in the Kazan region. Enrolled in 1874 in the Simbirsk Chuvash school. At the request of Ivan Yakovlev, Okhotnikov gave lessons in 1886 and 1887 to V.I. Ulyanov (Lenin), preparing him for his 'certificate of maturity'. In 1888 he entered the faculty of mathematics and physics at Kazan University. He died of tuberculosis before completing his final year.

One of the first Chuvash writers, author of the classic 'Notes of a Chuvash about his Upbringing', he was also a gifted mathematician (in 1891 his work was awarded a gold medal at a competition of the Society for Physics and Mathematics at the Sorbonne).

Feast days

I

In our village the festivals of the Orthodox church are hardly ever celebrated in the manner laid down by the Church. The Christian festivals have been transformed into pagan ones in the minds of the Chuvash, and instead of going to church, they stay at home to pray and remember the dead according to pagan rituals, and then begin feasting and making merry with their guests.

The children have a merry time at these festivals too. I have particularly happy memories of the festivals when we had guests. I used to wait for the day impatiently. Indeed, knowing our attitude to festivals, instead of exhorting us directly to work harder, the grown-ups used to say: 'Work with a will, children, and as soon as all the work is done it will be a feast day'. And the work went on apace. In the evenings, coming home from the fields, we sang songs appropriate to the coming festival, and quite forgot our tiredness. The songs we sang were Chuvash ones, but above all Tatar ones, which seemed to us more poetic. This shows incidentally that the Tatar influence on the Chuvash people of our village extended to the language. In fact, I was not a great lover of songs, though I

102

never refused when I was asked to sing with the others. Being taciturn by nature, I sang unenthusiastically, following the lead of the other singers. I was ten or eleven years old at that time, and was beginning to be guided in my actions by the opinions of my elders.

In this way a joyful mood of expectancy is established before a festival, for example that of Semik, and that of the Presentation of the Most Holy Mother of God. Two weeks before the latter began, my brother would go off to our relations living in other villages to invite them to a feast. Everyone in the house busied themselves with preparations for the festival, brewing beer, killing sheep and pigs. Work was found for me too in these preparations, and I did it gladly. On the eve of the festival, we all put on our festive clothes. I put on a crimson shirt, blue breeches, white woollen stockings and new bast shoes, and then, wearing a fur coat, a sheepskin cap and mittens, I went out with my brother to the gate to meet the guests. Recognizing one of them from far off, we would run to meet him, get into his sleigh with him, ride up to the front door, help him out of the sleigh, and quickly take his clothes into the house. Then we unharnessed the horse, tethered it somewhere and ran out to meet the rest.

Late that evening, when all those who were invited had arrived, there was the 'treating'. First my brother and I poured beer into beakers and went up to the guests, beginning with the old people, asking them each to drain a beaker. They took it from us, and we knelt down in front of them and remained in that position until all the beer was drunk. The other guests sat quietly meanwhile and watched the children treating. Only the person who is holding a beaker addresses the children. They are expected to behave politely towards guests, especially when treating them, since this involves persuading the guest with great politeness to drain the beaker. The ability to treat a guest politely and ingeniously is the mark of skill in treating. Afterwards the guests judge the mental powers of the children according to their success in this art. In order to test the treater, they sometimes refuse beer, saying that they have stopped drinking it because of illness or some other compelling reason. The ingenious boy in this case pretends to believe and sympathize with the guest, but suggests beer as a relief and a remedy. Eventually the guest appears persuaded by his arguments, thanks him for his kindness and sympathy, and gives the children small change to the value of two, three, or up to five copecks. But according to Chuvash custom, only guests enjoying a good reputation and the respect of the people, guests such as old Elmi, can test the children in this way. The others, when they have drunk up the beer and expressed their thanks, immediately give the treater a present.

When we had been round all the guests with beer, their real treating would begin, and I had to go off into the other half of the hut or on to the stove bed, from where I would watch the guests. They all sat round tables on benches spread with rugs and talked among themselves of everyday affairs, work at home and in the fields, the health of the cattle and of their families, the harvest and so on. On the table stood a pail of beer, a bottle or some other receptacle containing vodka, and one glass for the whole table, and then there was a dish of *tvorog* (curd cheese) around which lay pieces of black bread or slices of a home-made white loaf made from sifted wheaten flour. There were no napkins, forks or knives on the table apart from the bread knife. Instead of napkins, there was one common towel for everyone, lying on the table next to the pail of beer, which was often covered with the same towel – and instead of knives and forks there were hands and fingers. In addition, the guests were given tea in the morning, tea specially bought for feast days, but this only happened among the prosperous, who offered breakfast, dinner and supper. Breakfast, like dinner and supper, consists of soup, or *shchi* (cabbage soup) with beef, or *kasha* (porridge) or roast *shirtan*. This last is a kind of sausage, a Chuvash speciality made of beef.

The feast goes on for three days, and all the time the guests are treated with vodka and beer. First one member of the family goes round all the guests, offering them beer, and then another takes round the vodka. The Chuvash are very insistent in offering drink; they will not take back the glass or beer beaker until it has been drained. Such is the rule for all proper hospitality. When the guests get drunk, some start boasting about their wealth or their hard work, and others sing songs. The songs have a long-drawn-out, doleful melody. There is nothing dashing about them. The feast day has come, all the family has gathered together, they feel lighter in spirit, and under the effect of vodka tongues are loosened. They begin to comfort one another with words such as these: 'God will help us, we will live quietly, come here and let us eat and drink'. Those were my grandfather's favourite words when he had guests. He would often say: 'My friends, if there is something good in this world, it is to drink and eat and talk with your own people, all together as we are now'. After saying this, he would usually shed a few tears and continue: 'I have lived in the world, and I have never discovered anything more pleasant; live, young people, and may God give you health'. And when he was a guest at his sister's house, he was given a seat in front of everyone. Bowing their heads before him, two of his nieces, his sister's daughters, would kneel down and begin singing songs as they handed him a beaker of beer. They sang in the same way when they were seeing him off. The melody varied according to the contents of the song. These songs told of the carefree life of girls in their family home, their uncertain fate in the future, and their prayers to parents, relations and other elders not to regard them as strangers once they left the family nest. At this point the tune would become sad, grandfather would begin weeping quietly, and his nieces, Marya and Ulyana, had to keep wiping their eyes on the sleeves of their shirts. Then they would get up and go off quickly to another hut. I never saw what they did there, perhaps they wept or just sat there, but even when grandfather stopped weeping, they did not come out again to join the guests. The horse was ready, we got dressed and went out to the sleigh, where I would see Marya and Ulyana for the last time. They would be cheerful now, and would sit beside us in the sleigh, or go a long way with us. When we parted, there was no kissing or shaking hands. They just said: 'Keep well till we meet again'.

II

All these festivals have a religious element in them. In all of them the dead are remembered. I will give a brief description of the remembering of the dead at once such festival, the Presentation. The Chuvash have harvested all the corn in the fields. Autumn is beginning. The work of the harvest was preceded by various religious rites; *kasha* was made 'in honour of the rain' and the *uydyuk* and *khytdyuk* prayers were said. Now the harvest has been brought in. There must be more prayers to God, thanking him for this safe harvest. But the Chuvash does not want to be alone in his thanksgiving, he wants all his family, his departed grandfather, his father, his brother etc. to take part. When he invites his living relations to a feast, he also invites the dead. He remembers them, he wants to live with them again as once they all lived together. A time came when some of them no longer lived here. But the thoughts of the dead continue to exist, and now their descendants are carrying out what they had planned. 'Ah, if your grandfather was alive, he would be happy to see his grandson doing what he dreamed of doing long ago', says the Chuvash. He remembers the dead man and invites him to the feast, so that they can eat and drink their fill together and so express to God their contentedness and satisfaction.

Now the living relations have come and are sitting in their places. The dead are not yet in the house. But they will soon be amongst us, though invisible. All the talk has died down, except perhaps the squeaks of some uncomprehending small child, and even he will not be allowed to cry. The table is already set up near the door. There is a large dish on it. Around the dish are spoons, one for each dead person. There are also pancakes, a pail of beer with a beaker, and a pie containing chicken and vegetables. A large wooden beam is fastened to the wall opposite the door. There are wax candles burning on it, one for each dead person. So as to allow the departed into the hut, the door is slightly ajar. A feather mattress is laid out for them on the plank bed, and thick felt on the benches round the table – or failing that, there is a coat with the fur side up, or if the householder is really poor, a tunic.

Now all the family is gathered together, the living and the dead. The living are visible, the dead invisible. They are sitting unseen at a separate table. Then the oldest

106

member of the family goes up to the table of the dead and picks up a pancake which he breaks into pieces, putting one on each dead person's plate. As he does so, he names him, not by name, but by his family relationship: 'Here you are, grandfather, I remember you, enjoy the bread and salt of our hospitality.' In this way, he goes through all the departed, and as he does so, the tears run down his face. Then he picks up a pie and does the same thing. Then he pours a little beer into the plates, repeating the same words but saying 'beer' instead of 'bread and salt'. Finally he sits down at the table and tastes all the food and the beer. Thus he takes part in the feasting together with the dead. And thus they are remembered by everyone, in order of seniority. At such times you can often hear the guests sitting in their places and whispering to each other about the good things done by a dead person. When the commemoration is over, the plate, which is by now full of a mixture of bits of pancake, pie and beer, is carried out and emptied in the yard or street. The Chuvash are convinced there is no nourishment in these left-overs; it has been invisibly absorbed by the dead. What could be done with the food, if it were not thrown out? The dogs gather and pick up the scraps of bread. Having thus received the dead with the hospitality of bread and salt and the produce of their land, the Chuvash see them off, blowing out the candles, putting away the table and the benches and closing the door. Then begins the feasting of the living guests, as I have already described it.

(from 'Notes of a Chuvash about his Upbringing', 1888)

Kerkuri Filippov
(Kerguri Filippov)
(died 1914)

Filippov's ballad 'The Life of a Poor Man . . .', with its wealth of unusual images and unexpected associations, is one of the most original works of pre-Revolutionary Chuvash poetry.

Only at the end of the 1980s did any information become available about Filippov. He was born in the village of Takhartaga in the Yedrne district of the Kazan region. He was a village teacher, and subsequently a priest. His teacher was the outstanding Chuvash linguist and ethnographer Nikolay Zolotnitsky. On his advice, the poet-priest composed and published in 1874 a 'Life of Saints Gury, Varsonofy and German, with an account of the martyr Avraamy the Bulgar'. He also published anonymously various materials on Chuvash folklore.

The life of a poor man is the life of a hare in the fields

It was close on Easter time,
Food and logs were almost gone;
With an axe in my belt I set off
On the Khumzur road to the forest.
I reached the forest and night fell.
The wind said: *vash-vash-vash*,
And the treetops: *kash-kash-kash*.
A spring wind, a sharp wind,
A cold wind and a liquid wind,
Liquid but not sherbet –
Wherever it goes, it pinches.
What a life! What shall I do?
Light a fire – there's no fuel,
Wrap myself up – there's no blanket,
Go home – there's no way home.
The forest has eyes, the field has ears,
And the forest heard of my torment,
And answered me, and things grew easier,
And I took heart and approached it,
Approached the forest, stood before it.

I stood before it, but it was not a home:
Inside the oak something is talking,
Perhaps with me, but not in men's language.
I'd go in, but there's no door,
I'd take heart, but there's no-one to talk to.
I listen to that voice
And I am sad it's not a man's voice.
Eye may see, but tooth cannot bite,
And they say: You whip the shafts,
If you cannot whip the horse –
Thus frozen-souled and desperate,
I set fire to my soul.
The oak was before me, I had an axe,
I took counsel and struck the oak.
It cracked loud and split wide open;
And out flew the *arzyuri*,
Out he flew wailing.
And the forest started murmuring, groaning.
And the world grew suddenly dark,
And darkness covered my eyes.
My soul trembled with fear
Like a shuddering mare.
Such terror pierced my soul
That it drove out all the cold
That was lurking inside me,
And opened my eyes wide.
I would understand – but cannot,
I would walk – but have no strength.
What kind of a forest? – a nothing!
Not even a bundle of logs for me!
It just tore at my face,
And it whipped up my hair,
Not sparing my poor clothing,
It left me only tatters.
I rushed to right, and then to left,
Hither and thither on the snow,
And came out in the open fields.
The moon is shining brilliantly,
All is white – in utter infinity.
I did not see some field goat,
But suddenly a white fence,
And then a village full of people,

109

And my farm with all my household.
And I thought I had come home,
Came close, and there was nothing.
Only the road is shimmering
With the tracks of sleigh runners,
And further down the road
An icy film is crumbling,
And an empty sleigh is waiting;
And the wind moves it gently
One way and then another.
And I am in the sleigh,
And it glides in the same way,
Knocking at the road's edges,
Stopping and starting.
And ahead it is infinitely
Empty, infinitely white.

Sitar Ekhrime

(Ekhrim Sidr)

(1846–1921)

'A hook-nosed man with one eye. When a friend and I went to see him, we found him sitting in a hut without a chimney, making a bast sandal' – that is all we are told about Ekhrim Sidr by the writer who noted down this illiterate peasant's poems.

His work is very unusual among the Chuvash poetry of his time. Going against the tradition of Chuvash prosody (basically the line of seven syllables), he uses lines with different lengths and stress patterns, and makes bold references to 'crude' reality.

He was born in the village of Kiv-Sereshkel in Tataria and died during the great Volga famine.

They said Migikhver . . .

They said Migikhver had hanged himself,
And I too went to see.
There he hangs.
I stop and stand like a post.
He hangs, turning this way and that.
The eyes are wide staring.
The rope is firmly knotted,
The tongue bitten nearly at the root.
And I say to him:
'Oh, Migikhver, Migikhver!
Yesterday you were with the guests
With your arms around them,
Drunk with vodka,
And you killed yourself for slander.
Oh, Migikhver, Migikhver!
Your neck was soft, the rope thin,
See how it has bitten in.
You were saying goodbye to your family,
Now you say goodbye to the world.
Yesterday your soul was a soul,
Among people you were a person.

And now you lie silent
Like a rock at the foot of a hill.
As we carried out the body,
Suddenly lightning struck,
The body was hurled to the ground.
Thunder crashed time after time.
Everyone fled, they abandoned the dead man.
They stand and stare
And no-one dares come near.

Ivan Yurkin

(Ivan Yurkin)

(1863–1943)

One of the first Chuvash prose writers; a collector of folklore. His stories appeared in print in 1917. Before the Revolution he was able to publish five small volumes of Chuvash folklore with the help of the Turkologist N.A. Ashmarin.

He was born in the village of Pyurkel in the Buva district of Tataria. He attended the Chuvash school in Simbirsk, but the extreme poverty of his family forced him to leave and return home. He worked as a clerk, a bookkeeper and an exciseman.

Ourine
(Introduction to the story of that name)

Ourine is at the age when girls start going out to *posidelki* with their embroidery, she is a beauty with a face as pure as spring water, a warm heart, a small mouth, and the lips of a child. Her plaited tresses are pure and even, like her pure soft hands. And how modest her glance is, how innocent the pure black gleam of her eyes! Her fingers are pure and soft as white foam – such whiteness, like the tender brilliance of foam! It is as if they have never touched our black earth, never known the work by which our people live. But no, she is familiar with all kinds of work, yet her pure young body conquers everything and tells all the time of its beauty, purity and whiteness. And how fragile and delicate her bearing is! How all her movements contribute to her modest, innocent charm, the movements of her beautifully sculpted head, the movements and the trembling of her little hands, the movements of her back, quiet as ripples on the surface of a spring! And how fine our Chuvash costume looks on such a beautiful girl! How all the different colours answer one another! The light blue stripes on the homespun blouse stop short at the whiteness of the *sappun* [apron], and what a warm radiance there is in the tops of her bast shoes, and above them how fresh and clear the whiteness of the linen stockings – the

tala as the Chuvash say. And how the noise and shaking of
her necklaces harmonizes with all this! The coins on her
tevet and her *tukhya* gleam like the ripple on spring water,
resounding in harmony. The little eyes of the rings on her
fingers are eyes of agate and pearl – how tenderly and
warmly they look out!

Where, in what distant land, could you find such
beauty, modest and innocent, as if blessed by nature!

And if you see Ourine at work, you could faint at the
sight; so many kinds of human beauty will astonish you,
revealing themselves one after another. How tenderly soft
the rapidity with which she stretches the skein of tow over
the comb of the distaff! Now her left hand is pulling at the
tow, rapidly spinning it, while the right hand has set the
spindle moving so fast that it starts to sing, as if it had
received a friendly, talkative soul, and Ourine taps it
tenderly to hasten its movement. And her right hand
moves quickly, now sideways, now upwards, spinning
out the thread wonderfully evenly. The spindle jumps
down from the hem of her skirt on to the floor, and then
how it hums on the boards, like some hop-o-my-thumb
that has come alive in the wood! . . . It dances around the
floor, then up again on to the skirt! And all around the
skirt, gleaming like silver, fine threads of hemp are
scattered.

'Ah! – thinks Ourine joyfully, – ah, if only I can spin a full,
full spindle tonight! How many skeins of thread there
would be before Shrovetide and the happy sledging down
the hills, if I could work every day with the same joyful
inspiration! . . . Summer will come, and there will be still
more joy! I shall bleach some of the yarn, and the rest will
be woven directly into cloth . . . I shall dye some of the
woven cloth my favourite colour, sky blue, and some of it
will go into the many-coloured blouses . . . And if I am
blessed to be sought after in marriage, some pieces of cloth
will be for presents to the family of my betrothed, others
for my wedding dress, and others for the first clothes I
shall give to my future husband' – and joyfully, with a
cheerful tap, Ouriné hastens the movement of the turning
spindle, and the maple-wood comb of the distaff,
accepting with joy the effort of work, hums and sings: *kirr-
kirr!* – as if the hollow inside a maplewood fiddle had been

114

awakened into life. And again, spurred on by the singing, the spindle jumps down to the floor, now humming, now cooing, now snorting, showing where the floor is rough and where it is smooth. What a lot of different joys – for things and for human souls – come together in this festive work!

Ourine, joy of my heart! How I wish I had the skill to take part in this festivity! How I too, sitting beside you with my spinning wheel, would keep urging my spindle on – and my work would rival yours, joy of my heart! . . .

(1916)

Kheveter Turkhan

(Khevéder Turkhán)

(1876–1934)

Born in the village of Turkhan in the Yalchik district. Younger brother of the poet Yakku Turkhan. Attended a religious school for day pupils for four years, but remained a peasant. He lived all his life in his native village, and died in a tree-felling accident.

Turkhan is one of the first Chuvash writers to produce lyrics of personal feeling and experience; his poetry contains a number of prosodic innovations.

The spring flower shines

The spring flower shines in the field: *yal-yal!*
    The lark's voice flows through the field;
Over the petals wafts the wind: *vash-vash,*
    The wind's voice grows quiet and calm: *var-var,*
The lark's voice rings in the heavens: *yan-yan,*
    The wind wafts it down to us: *vash-vash.*
The lark's two wings are a-flutter: *var-var,*
    I look up to heaven and see them.
The lark's little voice is sad, very sad,
    We cannot tell what poems it sings.
Without words the singing speaks to us –
    My heart hears, and is plunged in thought.

(1898)

In the wide field

In the wide field how white the birch!
Like white, white snow amidst the green;
And in the green is an unending song,
The nightingale's song of grief.

How can I know what the nightingale thinks,
How can I make its thoughts mine?
If I could, I should weep with the tears it sheds
And comfort myself with its comfort.

But I cannot be there amidst the green,
Though I gaze on it in the wide field.
One thing is mine, to suffer from its song
And never to know its thoughts.

(before 1900)

117

Kerkuri Timofeyev

(Kerguri Timofeyev)

(1878–1938)

Born in the village of Terlemes in the Kuslavsk district. He attended the Chuvash school at Simbirsk until 1890 and became a teacher in the Buva district of Tataria. After making a thorough study of the history, customs and manners of the Chuvash of this area, Timofeyev composed between 1896 and 1903 his classic ethnographic work (*Tkhryal*). Even though this book has been constantly used by students of Chuvash history, language and folklore, it remained in manuscript for many years, and was only published in its entirety in 1972 (a few extracts were printed in 1908). From 1925 Timofeyev taught in Chuvashia and from the end of the 1920s in Siberia. Arrested in 1937 on a charge of 'nationalism', he died in prison.

All creatures and all things

All creatures and all things in the world have souls like us; they all think, as we do, and like us they feel cold and heat, good and evil, but they have a different language from ours. All things, all animals, wild beasts, birds – everything in the world – all speak a language that is understood by their fellows; and because they do not speak in human tongues, we cannot know what they think or how they live. Only occasionally is there a man who knows their language, but he is forbidden to communicate it to others. He only reveals his secret on his deathbed, or shortly before. And he only tells it to those who are like him. There are few such people, but in this way they pass on their art to one another and preserve it. They must not even show the animals that they understand their speech; in such cases, the animals turn from them in anger, reproaching them and weeping: 'Do not reveal our thoughts to men!' – for they say they suffer greatly because people understand their language. It is said also that the same is true of the language of things. But man has more to do with the animals, so he speaks more often of animals. Lest the animals should suffer, it is forbidden to speak of them in their presence. For knowledgeable people know that they

118

are acquainted with our language and understand our conversations. Children, insects of all kinds, birds, animals and all other creatures and things are all pure, 'blessed', 'sinless', 'innocent' beings. They must not be talked about; it is feared that the power of words might harm them. And not only that – they must not even be looked at with any sort of desire, man must not lust for them with the eye, for the eye of man can easily become the evil eye. Therefore, if our Chuvash speaks of animals, it is always with caution, sparingly and tenderly. If he is obliged to ask questions about them, he will only dare ask those nearest to him. In such cases, he will say something like: 'Is this possible, is this the right way, or should it be a little different'? The person who is questioned, even though he knows the questioner, begins by considering the question in silence, thinking whether it is asked with good or evil intent, 'with grace' or 'without grace'. Only after doing so will he answer; to the person who has 'grace' and is capable of blessing the living, he will answer to the point; to the indifferent person without the 'fire of grace' he will answer 'through his teeth', but will whisper to himself as he does so: 'May a branch put out your eye!' or 'May you be struck blind!' But to the greedy or malicious person he will answer nothing at all, and will turn the conversation in another direction. In such cases, the other man will not continue his questions either. In general the Chuvash avoid such talk; they are afraid of looking at something or somebody with desire and avoid casting a covetous eye on living or non-living beings. They are always mindful of the 'possibility of receiving grace', of being 'blessed', and they say: 'At such and such a time, by the highest blessing, such and such a thing happened', 'there is an unknown power that warms the soul. This power can sense the presence of a soul', or else, 'what the soul feels, is fated to happen'. And they add: 'On a person's shoulders sit two angels – *pireshti* – one on either side, one of evil, the other of good.'

(from *Tkhryal*)

119

Kaverle Fyodorov

(Kaverle Fyodorov)

(1878–1962)

In 1929 it became known that there was a peasant singer who possessed a remarkable musical memory and knew several hundred folk songs. Kaverle Fyodorov was brought to Cheboksary, where some 150 of his songs were written down and published by the composers F. Pavlov, S. Maksimov and V. Vorobyov. Then in 1949 Maksimov (rehabilitated after many years in the labour camps) started working with Fyodorov again and recorded another 470 melodies. A volume entitled 'Chuvash Folk Songs, 620 Songs and Melodies Recorded from Gavril Fyodorov' was published in 1969. Fyodorov's songs have become widely known and their authenticity admired by musicologists of several countries.

Kaverle (Gavril) Fyodorov was born in the village of Tomakassi in the Cheboksary district. He attended parish school for about two years, but from the age of 14 he travelled about, working at different times as a carpenter, a loader and a barge hauler on the Volga. During the Soviet period he lived in his native village, working on the collective farm.

My songs

As a boy of five or of six years old,
I took out my songbook, my precious bag;
I have kept it safely until today,
Filled it with seven hundred songs.

I cast a net into the Volga
To catch the white salmon;
The white salmon was caught, it leapt
As I hauled my net from the water.

I dreamed about the days to come:
Was it any use my singing?
Now I see that it was some use
For fame's music echoed around.

The new sleigh is gleaming.
The sleigh runs forward,
Leaves a bright trace shining.

120

This song that I sing you,
May it ring through the village
And my fame remains shining.

On the ring of silver
There are patterns and symbols,
Wear the ring till they wear out.

And the songs I have sung,
Remember them and sing them,
Till they wear out of memory.

(1950)

Taras Kirillov

(Taras Kirillov)

(1880–1921)

Born in the village of Sesmer in the Yedrne district. Graduated from teachers' training college and missionary school in Kazan in 1903. Was a priest from 1905 to 1918 and thereafter a teacher in the Nizhegorod region. Died of tuberculosis. Between 1905 and 1916 published five small books of poetry which reveal his deep religious feelings.

Song of the peasant about his work
(extract)

I

Treasure of my soul, grey horse,
You are with me in my work.
While you are in health, together
You and I do the autumn ploughing.
Let my children harvest the oats
Standing alongside their mother.
But you, grey friend, come with me
And plough the fields for winter corn.
And the days were so scorching
That the sand burned and fired the soul.
And the peasant's heavy labours
Melted into his hot blood.
But all the while we did not notice
How the time was slipping by –
Now the sheaves have all been carried
In to the threshing floor,
And the children's souls are already
Gladdened by the apple orchard,
The people are preparing the festival,
And further off, in the same garden,
It looks like the first hoar frost . . .
Bunches of hops are hanging down.
But we shall gather them, even in rain,
Gaily whistling to ourselves.

No, until the child starts crying,
The mother will never feed him;
And the house will never be warm,
If the peasant's hands are without work.
I bought bast for forty copecks,
Shall I make a profit from it?
I brought my *lapti* to the bazaar,
Will the bazaar ever be mine?
It is all we have, the *lapti*
Of lime bast always on our feet;
Put them on at dawn, and off at sundown –
So time slips away unnoticed.
Oh, my life, unnoticed life,
Hidden you are, but dear to me,
For thus we are, we have no desire
To go chasing after profit.
And then we don't know how to read,
A laughing stock for other folk . . .
But this we have for our comfort,
That people expect from us
No more than just ourselves.

(1912)

Nikolay Shelepi

(Nikolay Shelebi)

(1881–1945)

Born in the village of Sene Yuzel in the Aksu district of Tataria. His grandmother and grandfather were famous folk singers. In 1895 he left primary school, then worked for ten years as a peasant. In 1905 he published revolutionary poems in a Chuvash newspaper, and in 1907, to escape from the police, he went to work in Siberia. In 1910 he began to work as a peasant again, writing poems in the Tatar language. In 1916 he was a soldier in the Tsarist army. After the Revolution he worked on the Executive Committee of the town of Chistopol, on the committee for poor relief, and in various cultural and educational organisations. In 1931 he lost his sight; in 1936 he was awarded the title of Chuvash People's Poet.

One of the features of old Chuvash poetry is the accumulation of descriptive detail; Shelebí gives a virtuoso rendering of this tradition, with a touch of humour.

Feast days
(from the poem 'Syaramzan and Khandarzya')

Warm mists are wandering,
Bringing forth mushrooms.
By the feast of dead souls
All earth's wealth has appeared.

And on to the fields already
Come lines of young men and girls,
Tenderly and gladly looking
Into one another's eyes.

Embracing one another,
They play the game of 'drinking mead',
And with moist lips
They kiss one another.

On the white skirts and dresses
Is stitching like flowers of the field,
Their young voices can be heard
Like flocks of swallows twittering.

With heads thrown back, like brother and sister,
They look in one another's eyes.
And the old men too are gathered
To take pleasure in their games.

And the singing and laughter
Are like waters flowing . . .
Far away, like white clouds
Are the mountains of Syaramzan.

With the whole people they celebrate
The common feast of dead and living,
And sorrow for days gone by
Can sometimes be heard in their songs.

And with broad steps, all together,
They circle around the villages,
And little by little disperse
Gently saying goodbye like brothers.

And still like the ringing of bells
Echoes of songs hang over the village,
Footsteps from festive shoes still shine,
But soon they will have gone . . .

(1915)

Nikolay Shupussynni
(Nikolay Shubussinni)
(1889–1942)

One of the founders of modern Chuvash literature, friend and ally of Kestenttin Ivanov. Born in the village of Ikassi in the Cheboksary district. Enrolled in 1905 in the Chuvash training school in Simbirsk. Expelled in 1907 for political reasons, he was employed from the autumn of that year on the translation commission of the Chuvash school – working in particular on the translation of the Bible. Qualified in 1909 as a teacher and worked in a village school.

Shubussinni took part in the First World War and the Civil War. After the Revolution he worked in a number of Soviet organisations, including the Collective Farm centre of the Agriculture Ministry in Moscow. He was arrested on a charge of 'nationalism' and died in a labour camp.

His first works were published in the anthology 'Stories and Traditions of the Chuvash' (Simbirsk, 1908). His most important work of the Soviet period is a long historical poem about the period of Catherine the Great, 'The Favourite'. His 'Short History of Chuvash Literature' (1930), written in Russian, is the first work of its kind. A collection of Chuvash tales recorded by him was published in Russian in 1937.

He had an excellent knowledge of the pagan folk poetry of the Chuvash, and there is often a mystical quality about his work. At the same time, he is the author of the first genuinely realistic Chuvash work, the long poem 'The Clang of Yandrak'.

The day of the Great Kalam
(Prologue to 'The Clang of Yandrak')

More golden than ever he was is the sun;
From the heavens, from unthinkable heights
Through the clouds he pours down his golden grace
On to all the living, all souls on earth;
His eyelashes flashing spread ever more wide,
As he drops from thin lips the sparks of his smile.

And the tent of the sky, incredibly blue,
Is boundless, unthinkably high above;
And the sun's light visibly comes to us;

Under the sun the few clouds are still;
Not even desiring to come together
As if each knew its place of eternal peace.

Why, sun, are you so full of light in this world,
As if your rays could never be quenched,
As if no obstacle could break your beams?
Are the souls and the joys of living creatures
In some way akin to your bountiful burning,
Do you too not rejoice in their company?

Does the song of the little lark arouse you?
Does the shepherd's pipe attract your thoughts?
Or does the trembling of human hearts
Find a trembling echo in your living fire;
Or, all-seeing one, and giver of sight,
Do you see in their eyes a fraternal love?

Village streets are full of you. When you light them
They are full of the whiteness of festive dress;
Freed from toil, people brim with the life of your beams;
Only here and there at the forest's edge
White tatters of melting snow skulk and hide –
And that too is a part of the common joy.

As they melt there is laughter and darting of rays,
The song of soft waters sweetens the feast-day;
Sun, our Great Kalam, with you we rejoice;
You are fullness of blessing, and we are filled,
The grass is green, the orioles are singing,
All are blessed in our common brotherhood.

(1907–8)

Melting snow

In bright shining the village laughs,
With chatter and shout comes the cry
   Of the spring.
The sun has charged out with a snort
And galloped with clatter and clang
   Into heaven.
The snow is white, grey, white,
Its one thought, its thought, is to sink
   To the warmth below;
It raves, grows confused, forgets,
Loses shape, loses form
   In the game.
Melts like butter, melts like thought,
Hiccups, belches and snorts
   To all ears;
It excites itself with its grief,
Confuses grief with joy,
   And it roars;
It hangs about its own neck,
Throws off its own adornments
   In the dance;
Calls its friends, from heaven, from earth,
And suddenly all is Life,
   One Life! –
And in the strength of this friendship
It smiles in Death, its Death!
   And vanishes.
Where is it? Where is its feast?
It is gone, and now there is only
   The Green, the Green!

(April 1926)

Ille Takhti

(Ille Tkhti)

(1889–1938)

Born in the village of Nyushkassi in the Urmar district. Graduating from the Kazan training college in 1908, he became a village school-teacher. From 1922 to 1925 he was an inspector in the Ministry of Education of the Chuvash Republic. From 1925 to 1928 he studied at the Moscow Literary Institute, then became a professional writer in Chuvashia, and is known as a master of Chuvash prose. In the last years of his life, he was subjected to fierce literary harassment. He died of tuberculosis.

Song of praise to the Chuvash poets

Rather than be a Chuvash poet,
Better to be an orphan boy;
Better to dress in rags and tatters
And wander through the streets alone,
With hand outstretched, and bag to gather
Rubbish and leavings, skin and bone.

Rather than be a Chuvash poet,
Better to be a rotting log,
A dried up stump of a perished tree
That the wind has tumbled into the bog;
Better by far to crash to earth
And be carried off by the waters of spring
To float downstream on the Volga's waves,
Tossed and rocked by the Volga's swirl,
And then at last to be born away
To the edge of the world.

Rather than be a Chuvash poet,
Better to be a rowan branch,
Better on some black autumn night
To set off into the forest trees,
Chasing the wood demon, the *leshy*,

To crush his bones and to hammer him,
Hunting him down all night till dawn.

Rather than be a Chuvash poet,
Better to be a jet black snake,
And when the quarrelsome Chuvash folk,
The envious little Chuvash folk
Are fast asleep and gaping wide
Their nasty quarrelsome snoring mouths,
To creep without sound between their jaws
To slither into their greedy throats,
To curl up there inside their guts
And close beside their envious hearts
To make a nest where the baby snakes
Can writhe and wriggle and stick their fangs
Out of the nest and bite their hearts
Day and night, so that venom like yeast
Will breed black envy for ever there.

Rather than sing this bitter song,
Better to give your hands something to do,
Better to take a good strong stick
And go out into the village street
And chase all the neighbour's animals,
Beating the first that comes to hand.

Rather than be a scribbler of verse,
Better to be a bedraggled crow
Scenting a death three days away,
Sniffing the smell of carrion,
To caw and croak at the black priest's window,
To tap your beak on his holy panes,
Gladdening him with a funeral,
Telling him to prepare his prayers.

Rather than toiling endlessly
Making a scrawl of tedious verse,
And wrinkling up the skin of your brow,
Better by far to be an owl,
Flying out hunting chickens at night,
Shrieking or hooting now and then
From the old willow-tree branch,

130

Sitting up there night after night,
Giving a fright to the thieving crow –
Cunning rogues always ready to snatch
All kinds of trash from here and there.
To sit in the tree and shriek and scare them,
Pointing out in the foggy night
Ways to travel down crooked roads.

Rather than be a Chuvash poet,
Better to be a fire-breathing dragon,
And when the sun has set, by night
Under the light of the waning moon,
With a skin of scarlet sparks,
And flesh like a burning coal,
To fly up against the sky,
Scattering flakes of flame,
And scorching with their heat
The hearts of the people of your tribe
As they lie asleep in their beds.

People who write in the Chuvash tongue,
Rather than stain with ink
Paper and points of quills,
Better to take knives and sharpen them
And start preparing the bast,
Pulling strips of lime across the shoetree
And set about making *lapti*,
Beating the bast with hammers,
And when the *lapti* are ready,
To sling them behind you on cords of bast
And set off on the road to market.
And then you can buy with the profit
Salt and kerosene that you need,
And if you can sell them for more,
You'll have money to buy tobacco.

You who have already stood forth
Before the whole Chuvash people
In expectation of honour to come,
You whose name is known to the world,
Chuvash writers of poetry,
Venerable elders, young men and children,

131

Better for you
To be posts!
Through the length and breadth of the Chuvash land
Stand there in rows in every village,
Stand at the entrance to every village
Like gateposts in the fields,
And when all the travelling people
Come walking or riding past
And slam the gates shut behind them,
Then cry out to all our country,
Striking the ends of the axles
Of the carts coming in and out –
And enjoy life endlessly.

(1925)

I van K urak

(Ivan Kurak)

(1889–1942)

Born in the village of Kive Kalatka in the Simbirsk region. Attended the
parish school and then art school in Astrakhan. In 1924 returned to
Chuvashia and worked as a peasant and a bookkeeper on a collective farm.
In 1937 moved with his family to Turkmenia and worked for the rest of his
life in art studios at Bayram–ali. Having published in 1926 a small book of
verse which obtained a permanent place in Chuvash poetry, Kurak wrote no
more poetry.

Rye

Oh, rye, my rye!
Why bow your head earthward?
Why waste your own beauty,
Your golden beauty weeping?

Why do you stare at me
With a beggar woman's eyes?
And why, as black as soot,
Do you scatter your riches?

Like gold you grew up tall,
Now you shrink, as black as coal;
Stripped bare as I watch you,
You need no knife to cut me.

You wanted winds . . . They are here,
Why then do you not greet them,
Or is it too poor for them,
An ear with just five grains?

And how the swifts shouted
And bustled above you!
They would have settled by you,
But there was no place for them . . .

Oh rye, my rye!
Like a fish seeking moisture,
Is it not in your power
To keep breathing for ever?

For you know that man's life
Is an unending struggle,
Without this he would never
See the clear light of day.

And I – I will gaze at you
And catch you by the ears,
I will teach myself agronomy
And take you in hand.

Together with your friend
The clover I will sow you,
And your ears will ripen
And then I will make hay.

And you will greet me,
Standing taller than my head,
And your ears will hang earthwards,
Longer than plaits.

And I will stroke your head
With a hand no longer bony,
And smile on you with a face
Rich and blooming with blood.

(1924)

Kestenttin Ivanov

(Kestenttin Ivanov)

(1890–1915)

Kestenttin (Konstantin) Ivanov was born in the village of Slakpus in the Belebey district of Bashkiria, the son of a rich and literate peasant. In 1903 he entered the Chuvash school in Simbirsk, and in 1907 was expelled together with some classmates for a political strike. In the autumn of that year, Ivan Yakovlev invited him back to Simbirsk to work on the Chuvash translation commission (he translated the 'Song of Songs' for the Chuvash Bible). He was a day pupil at the Simbirsk classical *gymnasium* until 1909 and in the autumn of 1910 began to teach writing and drawing in the women's section of the Chuvash school of Simbirsk. More details of his life will be found in the Introduction, pp. xxviii–xxix.

Narspi, the long narrative poem which made him famous, was published anonymously in Yakovlev's 1908 anthology 'Stories and Traditions of the Chuvash'. It has since been published several times in Russian, has been translated into several of the languages of the USSR and published in separate editions in Bulgaria and Hungary. Apart from this poem, Ivanov also wrote two long legendary poems, a number of shorter poems and an unfinished verse drama. His work gave definitive form to the Chuvash literary language and established new poetic norms, close to those of European literature.

A monument was erected to Ivanov in Cheboksary in 1952. The Chuvash theatre of music and drama bears his name, and in 1966 the Chuvash government established a Kestenttin Ivanov Prize for literature and the arts.

Narspi

(extract)

In the steppe amid the green grass
Grows a bright yellow buttercup.
In the great village of Silbi
Grows a girl, the young Narspi.
She has a luminous, tender face
Like the yellow flower of the field.
And her eyes are deep black,
Like black agates they shine.
Curly plaits of hair entwined

Swing gaily at her back;
And when she walks lightly by,
Necklaces ring at every step.
She has but to shoot a glance
And the young man's heart beats faster;
She has only to give a smile
And the young man's soul is softened.
Who can look on the meadow flower
And not feel his eyes burn bright?
Who can see such a girl
And not greet her with a sigh?

* * *

As soon as the sun has gone to rest,
She briskly washes and dries herself,
And goes to join the choral dance
With a *shyulgeme* on her breast;
A *tevet*, ringing *shigr-shigr*
Is hanging from her shoulder;
A red silk kerchief, maiden-like,
Is tied in a knot around her head.
And in the choral dance her voice
Is like the voice of a rare bird,
But when she laughs with all her heart,
You would say: ah, she is strong.
Until the choral dance is done,
This voice cheers the dancers on . . .
And now the morning star is rising,
Smiling light from the sky's depths.
And Narspi, in her father's house,
Is sleeping peaceful and untroubled;
Dreaming only happy dreams,
She is happy too in sleep.

* * *

Up with the dawn, Narspi dresses –
Straight away she sets to work:
Singing, she takes a silver thread,
Embroiders patterns on the cloth,

Or else sits down to sew a seam
As even as a row of beads.
The steel dog with the scanty tail
Vanishes, then appears again;
And then she will sit down to weave,
How she can make her shuttle play!
Or else she takes the spinning wheel
And winds her distaff in a trice.
Perhaps the cat is on the bench
Starting to wash its face with its paw,
And here too Narspi is ready,
Preparing food and drink for the guests . . .
Yes, her life was well spent,
Till the time of maidenhood was done,
Till the time they came to her father's house
To marry her to a foreign man . . .

(1908)

(*shyulgeme* and *tevet* – adornments)

137

The iron brake

In our village long ago
I remember an old woman.
(Now she is lying in her coffin,
Sleeping in the cemetery.)
And an evil life she led,
This old woman. She had a cat,
A pair of sheep, and in the loft
Of her decrepit village house
She kept some owls. And there close by
Stood a brake for beating hemp.
In this brake, or so they say,
There was a white devil sitting;
Just lay a finger on the brake
And all his teeth would be chattering.
But if you started beating hemp,
He'd throw a stalk right in your eye,
And if the stalk stuck in your eye,
The woman would turn into a witch.
And then, they say, at the witch's bidding
The iron brake would gallop out
Through streets and over sleeping fields
Banging its beater as it went.
Then if anyone stood in the way
Of the brake as it came galloping,
The poor soul would be crushed to death
And his blood drunk – or so they say.
She was blind, this aged dame –
The devil with his hempen stalk
Had put out the old creature's eye
Because she had the iron brake.
And once you had lost your sight,
It wasn't hard to become a witch.
So the old woman was known
For a witch all the country round.
There was no-one who didn't know her,
Not a dog that didn't know her.
The old dame had a daughter-in-law,
Her name was Cheges, the swallow,
And truly she was like a swallow,
Magically beautiful,

138

With fingers nimble for all work
And lips that were soft for kissing.
Simple and sweet in everything,
She made the village people glad,
But her mother-in-law had no love for her,
For the old woman was a fool.

* * *

All the time young Cheges was asking
The old woman: 'Mother dear,
Let me go out visiting,
Let me go out, mother dear!
– Be off with you, leave me in peace!
You make me dizzy with your asking.
Work a bit harder – when it's time,
I'll let you go out visiting.'
But for three whole days Cheges
Kept on begging the old woman:
'Let me go out, mother dear!
Let me go to see my sister.
– Oh, may the serpent swallow you!
Be off, be off, I'm tired of you;
No-one can escape his fate,
Be off with you tonight, this minute,
Don't let me see you in the house!'

* * *

Hastily the girl prepared
A milky dough for three *yusmans*.
A *yusman*, you know, is a cake
Made and baked with magic spells
And invocation of good spirits,
And it possesses magic power.
Whenever someone from our people
Is setting out on a long journey
To protect themselves from evil,
They always carry a *yusman*.
And so our heroine one night
Harnassed a horse for travelling,
Went on a visit to Agar.

139

The iron beater bangs and clangs,
The old woman is beating hemp,
She opens the gate on its brass hinge,
Speaking a spell as she opens it:
'Bang and bang, my brake, and beat,
Gallop along the Agar road,
Catch my daughter-in-law, my brake,
Spoil her pretty head, my brake!'
With a clatter the iron brake
Gallops off along the road.
Hearing it come, the fair-haired girl
Strikes up a song, urges her horse:
'Light of the moon is lighting us,
The Agar road is smooth and bright,
Gallop, gallop, gallop, horse,
Go to the place I want, my horse,
Frighten, frighten my enemy,
Yusman which I make with milk!'
She throws one *yusman* in the air,
She leaves one *yusman* on the road.
Now the brake was very close,
But when it came to the *yusman*,
It started back, leapt in the air
And galloped back along the road.
'Bang and bang, my brake, and beat,
Gallop along the Agar road,
Spoil her pretty head, my brake!'
The iron brake clatters away
And once again approaches her.
Hearing it come, the fair-haired girl
Tearfully begins her song:
'The Agar road is smooth and bright,
Light of the moon is lighting it,
Gallop, gallop, gallop, horse,
Go to the place I want, my horse,
Frighten, frighten my enemy,
Yusman that I made with milk!'
And she throws on to the road
The last of her three *yusmans*.
The brake was almost up with her,

But suddenly stopped in its tracks,
Rooted there by the *yusman*,
Then galloped back along the road.

* * *

The girl has reached her destination
And hammers at her sister's gate:
'Sister, sister, let me in,
Let little sister Cheges in,
A fierce enemy is after me!
– I have no guests who come at night,
Off you go, get on your way!
– Fare you well then, sister dear!'
Cheges goes on her way and knocks
At her elder brother's gate:
'Brother, brother, let me in,
Let little sister Cheges in,
A fierce enemy is after me!
– I have no guests who come at night,
Off you go, get on your way!
– Fare you well then, brother dear!'
Weeping now, the fairheaded girl
Crawls in underneath a shed
And sobbing buries herself in straw.

* * *

'Bang and bank, my brake, and beat,
Gallop along the Agar road,
Catch my daughter-in-law, my brake,
Spoil her pretty head, my brake!'
The iron brake goes clattering off,
Flies into the village of Agar,
Galloping, clanking furiously;
Cheges's soul is filled with dread . . .

* * *

141

And the old woman by her gates
Is waiting, waiting for her brake –
No sign of it, it must have gone mad
Being so long in coming home.
It can be heard far, far away,
Clattering away along the road,
And the old witch in her confusion
Starts to call it, calls her brake:
'Bang and bang, my brake, and beat!
Now gallop home to me, my brake,
Come back home to me, my brake,
Come in under my roof, my brake!'
Far, far away along the road
Like a dragon hear it hiss –
It must have gone mad, it seems,
Fighting, struggling with someone,
Beating something, trying to break it.
'Bang and bang, my brake, and beat,
Now gallop home to me, my brake,
Come back home to me, my brake,
Come in under my roof, my brake!'
Far off, far off along the road,
You can hear cracking and crunching,
And the brake comes madly racing,
Making the whole earth shake beneath it . . .
It gallops up, the beater swings –
And the old woman's head flies off.
The blind old woman had no time
To take herself out of the way,
The brake came running at the gallop
And took her head off at one blow.

* * *

And now the long dark night is over,
Slowly, slowly comes the dawn.
Agar-yal awakes from sleep,
Now that the heavy night is gone.
Everyone comes out to work –
Such is the life of the Chuvash –
The brother of the girl Cheges
Going out to feed to his cattle,

142

Finds his little sister's corpse
Lying there beneath the straw.

                              * * *

And in our village street the people
Are all standing, gossiping,
And round about the old dame's corpse
They stand and stare and buzz like flies.
There she lies, without a movement,
And the black blood all around her,
In one place her body lies
And in another place her head.
And the brake stands, quiet now,
Not a sound beneath the eaves . . .
The people speak as with one voice,
But in a hundred different ways.

(1908)

(*brake* – metal implement with teeth and a 'beater',
used for beating flax or hemp)

Kheveter Pavlov

(Kheveder Pavlov)

(1892–1931)

Born in the village of Bayryal in the Tsivil district. In 1907 entered the Chuvash school in Simbirsk and was a close friend of K. Ivanov and N. Shubussinni. In 1922 he organized the music college in Cheboksary and was director of the Chuvash state choir. A year before his death he joined the Leningrad Conservatoire.

Pavlov is the most important Chuvash composer, founder of Chuvash symphonic music, music critic, poet and dramatist. He collected and arranged about 300 folk songs, and published a study entitled 'The Chuvash, and their Songs and Music'. He is the author of the classic drama *Yalda* (In the Village).

The girl and the violin

Good one,
Kindly one,
If you love me just a little
Hear my violin speaking . . .
        'For your radiant beauty
        My thoughts swarm like bees.
        On a dark day your image
        Lights the world like a sun . . .'

Is she good?
Is she kindly?
She hardly turns to look at me,
Shakes her golden head, not seeing me.
With her proud soul she troubles
My soul in its distress.

Good one,
Kindly one,
If you love me just a little,
Hear my violin speaking . . .
        'Powerless to resist you,
        I would weep as I embraced you.

I would gladly live my life
Simply gazing on you . . .'

Is she good?
Is she kindly?
Does she love me just a little?
Am I not a stranger to her?
My violin, tell me! . . .
But the violin is silent . . .

(Simbirsk, 1912)

Semyon Elker

(Semyon Elger)

(1894–1966)

Born in the village of Asla Ubakassi in the Ibres district. Attended village primary school before the Revolution. A private in the First World War, he was seriously wounded and captured. After the war he took adult education courses in Kazan, worked as a village schoolteacher, then as a journalist and newspaper editor. His verse tale 'Under the Yoke', the most important Chuvash epic poem, was published in 1931. He also wrote a long historical novel, stories and dramatic poems. In 1940 he was awarded the honorary title of Chuvash People's Poet.

Before the coming of the fugitive Chuvash
(from 'Under the Yoke')

Kushlavosh, common field of twelve Chuvash villages,
Lies snugly concealed on all sides by dense forests.
And this woodedness in its solemn tranquillity
Protects this place like some primeval spring.
Happy under the forests, it breathes freely, blessedly . . .
And the grandeur of the forest, untouched by mankind,
Had never yet been measured in its breadth and its limits.
Two hundred years ago, even the beasts did not know it.
And the stately pine trees, two centuries old,
Reached up skywards, knowing only the life of the sky,
And with regal grandeur they conferred together,
Never tiring of their lives on the face of the earth.
In their midst, in damp places, the silky, furry mosses
Shone intact in their purity till the depths of autumn,
Receiving deer's hoofprints, and wiping them with dew.
Close by were the fir-woods and the many-treed thickets,
Holding off the sunlight and keeping it from earth;
The enormous oaks, like forest patriarchs,
Rustled majestically, singing in unison,
And peaceful the bird song sounded in that rustling.
In ravines deep and cool as on the day of creation,
Water glittered in grass like the first created waters;
Firs, immensely tall, making music in the wind,

146

Stretched up and gazed over the spaces of the earth,
Like the heads of the churches and temples of the forest.
Bees, still unfamiliar with the race of men,
Knew only the families and tribes of flowers.
Before the coming of people, Chuvash people,
Who fled here from christening into an alien faith,
The bodies and the feelings of the ancient trees here
Knew neither iron nor the voices of men . . .
But even thereafter, peace was long preserved here,
Until to this refuge, shadowed round by its forests,
Came different people, with their *volosts* and offices,
Who made of this place, this creation of nature,
Another world, a world open to all eyes . . .
And then too the forests heard the weeping of man.

(1931)

The hungry year

From beyond the world's rim, poisonously red,
Climbs the blinding sun, not withholding its heat;
It climbs, and slowly its scorching rays
Begin to eat into village and field.

The peasants wait for the rain and watch
The suffering inflicted on pasture and hay;
But the land's sickness does not trouble the sun –
It stands unmoved, not restraining its heat.

From morning to night between north and east
Limply blows a dry, monotonous wind;
Every now and then a cloud fragment appears,
But soon melts, dispersed by the scorching breeze.

In field, over meadow, a darkening gust
Unexpectedly gathers from every side –
Before you can see, in a flash it soars
And batters against the roof of the world.

With dreary images midday comes,
More strongly blazes the bonfire-sun;
Irresistible brightness, a liquid flame,
Sucks the bosom of the meadows dry.

Thirsting for moisture, the grasses and flowers
Crumple and crush their petals and leaves.
There will be no mowing; the hay has not grown
Full height, but dried yellow from the root.

The river bank is dark; no splash of water,
No reeds, no rushes growing down below;
Only alders and willows as in former days
Still look down trying to see their face.

Day after day, the unyielding drought
Tires and torments the land's withered breast.
The peasant still labours stout of heart,
But coming hunger oppresses his soul.

He thinks of how to withstand this distress,
What force he can find to defeat his fate,
And all the time he is seeking some way
To rescue his loved ones from a hungry death.

Seeing cornfields burning, still uncut,
Even the young keep silent and hide,
At the time of joyful dances and games
Their voice is unheard in the empty street.

(1921)

Sespel Mishi

(Mikhail Sespel)

(1899–1922)

Born in the village of Kazakassi (now Sespel) in the Kanash district, in a poor peasant family. He was soon parted from his beloved father, who was exiled to Siberia for a crime committed in a state of severe mental disturbance. In 1918 he left the training college in Tetyushi (Tataria) and joined the Bolshevik party, being sent to Moscow on a propaganda course, during which he heard Lenin speak. After working in the Tetyushi regional legal commission, in the autumn of 1920 he was appointed president of the Chuvash Revolutionary Tribunal and moved to Cheboksary. The building of the Tribunal was burnt down in spring 1921, and Sespel was arrested on the strength of a slanderous denunciation. He was cleared of the crime, but expelled from the party and sent to Nizhny Novgorod.

Seriously ill from the bone tuberculosis which had affected him since childhood, Sespel went from Nizhny Novgorod to the Crimea, and after treatment worked for the Kiev military authorities. Being exempted from military service, he remained in the Ukraine, serving in the Oster district of the Kiev region. His forced separation from his native land, his growing illness and his experience of the Volga famines provoked a severe depression. He committed suicide in the village of Starogorodka, near Oster.

During his lifetime, less than a dozen of Sespel's poems and a handful of his articles were published. His first book of verse appeared in 1928. Since then, his poems have been translated into Russian, Ukrainian and several other European languages. Two novels have been written about him, and in 1969 the Kiev Film Studio made a film entitled *Sespel*. In 1967 the Chuvash government established a Sespel Prize for literature and the arts. For further comments on his work, see the Introduction, pp. xxix–xxx.

The Chuvash word

The time will come. And the Chuvash language will cut through iron. It will grow sharp, will be red hot steel. The time will come too for people to hear again the song of the Chuvash. Lovingly they will sing, the Chuvash, of clear sky, red sun and expanse of white light. In the Chuvash song the lark will sing in the pure heavens. In the Chuvash tongue the sea will roar, the deep forest rustle, and the boundless fields put on greenness. And the groan of ancestral grief will be heard from its depths, and joy will rise up before us. Nature and the world of man on the Volga's shores will ring out like the *gusli* – this will be the sound of Chuvash song, Chuvash words, Chuvash language. The Chuvash tongue will be a fire of live coals and a red hot steel.

From of old the Chuvash lived oppressed. What suffering, what trial did he not bear to preserve his language. Bowing his head, pulling down his cap, he sat silent among the nations. For fear of mockery, he spoke in a whisper. We were crushed, ground down, scattered throughout the world.

Swept hither and thither, we hid in the depth of the forests.

But in all his tribulations, his great griefs, the Chuvash did not lose his dignity; he carried his honour and his good name through to our time.

Century followed century. The Chuvash spoke quietly together. From all sides the language was harassed. But it lives, it survives unharmed. In the face of mockery it is living today. It lives! May it flourish in future! So with his word the Chuvash will make the thunder roar and call down the flame of lightning. This gives us assurance. We believe! The time will come!

The man who believes is happy.

We shall not forget how they mocked our fathers. The language which endured persecution will not disappear without trace. Until now the Chuvash word has gone unheard – now the Chuvash song will ring out, Chuvash verse and the Chuvash word will become the waves of the Volga, the roar of the forest, the music of the *gusli*. The Chuvash tongue will cut through iron, will become sharp steel.

There will be a time! The day will come!

And when the day comes, the Chuvash will remember the man who wrote this down and will say: 'Yes, he spoke the truth'.

(Tetyushi, 1920)

150

Chuvash! Chuvash!

Chuvash! Chuvash! . . .
                    Chuvash! Chuvash! . . .
Your sleepy fields,
Your quiet, humble, kind and tender,
Timid and gentle villages,
I cannot bring myself to love them.
Why is the Chuvash soul so timid
When a new Chuvash world is at hand?
Is this the time for yawning sleep,
For cosy warmth? . . . Is this the time?

Oh, how I wish that I could see
The true-born Chuvash bold and daring!
Chuvash! . . .
                    Rise up, spread out your wings!
Lift your eyes towards the sun!

The Chuvash mind must be like steel,
Cut ice, and when it hits rock,
Cut through the rock and strike out fire,
Be red-hot steel.

Chuvash! Chuvash! . . .
                    Chuvash! Chuvash! . . .
Fly like an arrow, sharp and piercing,
Fly whistling, hissing, fly, take aim
Take aim at the heart of the world, strike home.
And Chuvash heart, be a singing flame
Of courage! Hiss, boil up and seethe,
A cauldron, melting gold.

(Kiev, 1921)

151

Ploughing of the new day

The plough is moulded out of the dawn's blue light,
And the sun dances, harnessed in the shafts.
The New Day – golden head with yellow halo –
Walks out into the Chuvash fields to plough.

The iron of the New Day's plough, blood red,
Cuts clods of earth, and lays new furrows out.
Beneath these furrows the old Chuvash age
Lies down and buries itself and dies.

The New Day looks; he sees his golden plough
Crumble the dried fields to a fertile blackness;
The fathomless cold spring has sent its icy streams
To irrigate the emerald meadows.

The New Day with his hand of red-hot steel
Has taken from a red and yellow basket
Thousands of stars, hundreds of thousands of stars,
And sows them in the field . . . The morning ray
Drawn like a burning harrow through the fields,
Has spread them with a hundred thousand stars.

When the time comes for new shoots to spring forth
For the New Day from out of the black earth,
Like sunny cornfields, broad under the sun,
The fate of the Chuvash will rise up boldly.
Sparks of these cornfields, silver and gold like braid,
Will spread over the earth with radiant music.

The Chuvash of a great new age, new born,
His shoulders reared against the azure sky,
Will go into the fields of life in sun-lit garments,
The New Day will embrace him gently, gladly:
Strewing new flowers on his new road, before him rises
The rainbow of the *Internationale*.

(1921)

When night comes on

When night comes on from afar, when the shade of evening
Covers the fields with sleep,
When row upon row the ranks of varied thought
Come and gather in my mind,
Then transparent forms and masses of ancient times
Show themselves from afar.

Among the shapes and masses of ancient times
Is the face of the Chuvash land:
My motherland is hanging there, hanging all alone,
On a red and bloody cross.
From the charred and martyred Chuvash heart
Drips blood, fresh dripping blood.
Over the Chuvash head howls the black, dank day,
Whistling on every side . . .

When night is past, when from the East,
Shooting light through the world, forging dew into jewels,
The summer day comes close with its silver voice,
Then my loving eyes are made glad on every side
As my motherland is taken from the cross
And raised up from the dead.

(1921)

153

Build a bridge

The roads . . . On the roads, the bodies.
On the outskirts, heaps of dead bones.
Oh, heavy times, oppressive!
You
    who are still
          alive,
Over bodies and heaps of bones
To sunlit Tomorrow
Build a bridge.
Oh,
    build a bridge!
If I,
    all strength gone,
          fall,
Walk over me, trample me
With iron feet,
Boldly trample my heart.
Oh,
    trample me,
          break my neck!
If while the bridge is building,
I fall, all strength gone,
Then throw me under the bridge –
Down, down,
          throw me down!
Oh,
    throw me, hurl me down!
No time for tenderness.
The day of sweet songs is gone.
Ahead of us shines the Sun.
But this is the time of death.
Those whose eyes have no tears to weep,
Those whose soul is a stone,
Cross over the bridge!
There are two crowds of people:
The strong will cross the bridge,
And the weak
Be hurled down.

On the paths, by the road, the bodies.

Over wide acres of fields,
The heaps of dead bones.
You who are still alive,
Over bodies, to Tomorrow,
Build the bridge.

Ah,
    I am whispering.
Strength gone, shoulders weak.
Hey!
    throw me down,
Down, down, throw me down,
Hurl me under the bridge,
Ah,
    break my neck.

(1921)

Hungry psalm
(extract)

The bony hand of the Old Day
Has nailed my country to the cross;
The mouth of hunger, the dry teeth
Of famine gnaw, gnaw, gnaw my land.

Log huts, damp with the sweat of martyrs,
Grow stiff in wretched poverty;
In agony lie the hungry fields,
Lie sick, dried up, hard as a bone.

The Volga stretches wide and groans,
Her yellow waves like tattered rags,
Moans with an endless, heart-sick moan,
Lamenting the land in dry-eyed grief.

Bony hunger grips my country's heart,
Hope's bright flower is set in ice.
Drying, decaying in men's souls,
The new Song of Rebirth has died.

Sun, sun! When you were here, the pulse
Of a strong new song caressed my mind.
. . . I have lost my tongue . . . If my land is dying,
Who needs you, song of mine . . .

                                        Who? who?

(1921)

Henceforth
(The last drops of blood)

Henceforth, turned into stones, in heaps,
The warm word, frozen, has stuck in the throat,
From the forest top day's light has fled,
And death lies over the world henceforth.

Barefoot on to the Hill of Torment
They have led my Country, led her by the hand.
The bloody sweat of the walls of Cheboksary
Is held in my shattered heart henceforth.

All bloody – what is this in my hand?
I break it, turn it to dust, to meat,
Tearing the veins. It is my heart,
Mine, Michael Sespel's bloody heart.

Like a dog that has had its hide ripped off,
I shall beg a crust in a stranger's yard,
Some drizzly day I shall drop down dead,
Hungrily howling for Cheboksary.

Henceforth from my innards, dried up with hunger,
Will come only the groan of the cold graveyard,
My soul will be filled with a massive millstone
Henceforth, henceforth, henceforth . . .

(1921)

Scarlet, scarlet, scarlet poppies

Scarlet, scarlet, scarlet poppies, life
In your flower that summer new unfurled,
Raging winds rose up and spread you far and wide,
Sand has scorched the softness of the world.

Poppies with soft petals of shot silk,
Life in flower that summer new unfurled,
I your friend am far away from you,
Weak with hunger, creeping through the world.
Scarlet poppies fill my memory,
For my scarlet poppies still I grieve.

Poppies with damp glistening heads of flame,
Life in flower that summer new unfurled,
Will it once again come back to you,
Midday summer heat of the lost world?
Will your poor friend see you once again
In the garden carpeted with green?

Scarlet, scarlet, scarlet poppies, life
In your flower that summer new unfurled.
Raging winds rose up and spread you far and wide,
Your starving friend goes creeping through the world.

(1922)

Serafim Vasilyev

(Serafim Vasilyev)

(1903–?)

Vasilyev's work is a unique phenomenon in modern Chuvash poetry. In 1963 the poet's daughter, who knew no Chuvash, sent extracts of his work from Tadzhikistan to Chuvashia. They were printed in 1969 with a preface by P. Khuzangay, who described Vasilyev's long poem as 'a magnificent hymn to woman the mother'. However, the poet has remained unknown except for the following official letter sent in 1977 from the town of Tuymazy in the Bashkir Autonomous Republic: 'Serafim Vasilyev was born in 1903, in the village of Sukkulovo in the Yermekeyev district of the Bashkir ASSR. Until 1936 he was a member of a collective farm. After 1936 he was employed in the Bashkir textile works at Nizhnetroitsky in the Tuymazy district of the Bashkir ASSR. He worked as a wool transporter, then in the boiler house. In 1963 he retired with a well-deserved pension. S.A. Vasilyev is a veteran of the Great Patriotic War, in which he fought from 1942 to 1945. He takes no part in public life. He is religious, but causes no harm to those around him.'

Mother
(extracts from a long poem)

Oh Mother! of all the heart's wealth you spent on me,
I, taking it all, have not returned a hundredth.
When you were living, I did not take care of you,
Now I would take care of you, but you lie in the earth.

You rose at dawn, mother, and you washed my face,
You fed me with broth from a little bowl.
When you went to the river, or out to the hayfield,
I walked close behind you, as if I was your lamb.

When you had to hurry off to some place for a moment,
I very often did not want to stay behind,
Then you, perhaps, would pick up a switch,
And pretend to be cross and drive me back home.

Then, mother, through the little eye of the window,
I would stare after you and watch you go.
For you were sweeter than everyone, mother,
And my eyes were not dry until you came home.

159

Sitting me down by your side in the evening,
Speaking gently to me, you would teach me lessons:
'Do not use bad words', you would say to me,
'Try to keep out of puddles, try to be more tidy . . .'

You would tell me, you would beg me to be kind to people,
Always to behave with respect to my elders,
And kindly and quietly you explained to me
That I too must learn to help about the house.

'If you do this, then my life will be easier,
I shall work in the fields with my mind at rest.
As I work, my little boy will remain in the house,
Then run out at evening as the cattle come home.

Let him live and be healthy, and instead of his father
He will ride with the elders on the night watch.
He will go and help his father with the harrowing,
And together they will go to the forest for wood.

In the evening he will drive the cattle back home,
And before I get back from the harvest field
He will peel the potatoes, gather up kindling,
And saw and chop wood to burn on the hearth . . .'

Rejoicing in your son as he grew taller,
You feasted your eyes on him with eager hope,
But when you gave birth to me, mother,
You gave yourself only torment and grief.

Sometimes in your sorrow you would wipe away
The tears from your eyes, hiding them from me.
Ripping the hem of your girlish dress,
You sewed it into a shirt for my back.

And I, seeing the tears in your eyes,
I suffered, grieving in my childish heart.
'Let me just grow big', I would say to myself,
'I will let no-one do my mother any harm.'

Sweet it is to remember you in these verses,
How you bore me, how you were a mother to me,
How you spent all of your life in loving,
Your loving soul burning like the sun! . . .

160

Semyon Khumma-Chekes

(Semyon Khumma-Cheges)

(1903–1936)

Born in the village of Yenesh-Narvash in the Tovay district, in a poor peasant family. After attending village school, he worked in Kazan on the staff of the newspaper *Kanash*, at the same time studying in the agricultural technical school. From 1927 to 1932 he worked as a proof-reader in the Cheboksary printing unit, and thereafter as an editor. Together with I. Tkhti, Khumma-Cheges is the most important Chuvash prose writer, the author of numerous tales and stories.

Song

Behind the forest,
Behind the hills,
The sun had sunk.

My beloved Anyuk,
Uzyop's daughter,
Comes out to dance.

The geese in line
Came to the birch-tree –
Ga-gaak, they cried.

Kusma Kuboz
Squeezed his accordion
With flashing eyes.

In a singing circle
Go the young men and girls,
Smiling and smiling.

And so they sing
And so they dance,
The whole place echoes.

I could not resist it,
I joined the dance
And my face blushed red.

– Don't push, Vanyuk! –
Anyuk says to me,
But laughs as she says it.

(1922)

Viktar Rsay

(Viktor Rzay)

(1906–1970)

Born in the village of Kaval in the Urmar district. Having attended Kazan Pedagogical Institute, he worked all his life as a teacher of Russian language and literature in secondary schools in Chuvashia, Tataria and the Ulyanovsk region. Having published a small book of poems in 1925, which attracted a great deal of attention and provoked heated discussion, Rzay virtually stopped writing, with the exception of a small amount of prose and translations from Chuvash into Russian. His lyric verse shows the influence of Russian Imaginism.

I shall come flowing

In the blue sky walks the golden lamb,
Frisks in freedom and shines with joy,
While I sit here, my dark head bowed,
A withered flower of the autumn . . .

A peasant looks at me and smiles,
Sitting there pulling on his pipe.
On the green willow the nightingale
Embroiders patterns with fiery voice . . .

Peasant, why are you so full of joy,
Listening to the bird so gaily?
Why have you come to me so early,
To find me alone with no-one near?

Do you think of me as a son in the fields
And want to give me your daughter in marriage? . . .
Then joyfully, bubbling like water in spring,
I shall come flowing to your daughter . . .

I have often watched her in the garden,
Giving her the name of little berry . . .
When I first looked in her eyes, all shyly
Like a boy I hid behind the fence . . .

Since then, I confess, when I talked with her,
I have often been astonished, my friend.
Her looks, how her looks make me melt with joy,
And her heart is as precious as coral to me.

The girls of Cheboksary, though they leap and run,
And smear their faces with oil or clay,
They look like mushrooms on a bright day,
Rotting, however much they smile.

But if you consider me a poet
Of the fields, and give me your daughter, friend,
Joyfully, bubbling like water in spring,
Today I shall come flowing to your daughter!

(1927?)

164

My country

My country wears a white linen dress,
She has no cotton to wear.
The hide of the present is too tough,
Beneath it lies no warmth.

Yes, the weather today is rough,
Black things are loosed in it.
– Watch out, your days are numbered –
A voice told me before dawn.

This voice came hissing in the wind,
It called me out of sleep.
Bad luck all round, horse stuck in a drift –
Its saddle-girth has snapped.

I don't cry. What if I bow my head
On the field, as on my breast.
What of it if all traces break! –
I shall survive this storm.

(1926?)

Ille Tuktash

(Ille Tuktash)

(1907–1957)

Born in the village of Asla Tuktash in the Elek district, in a poor peasant family. Attended the Party school in Cheboksary. Worked as an editor in a publishing house and a research worker in the Chuvash Scientific Research Institute. He fell ill while fighting at the front in World War II and died of tuberculosis.

Tuktash was a dramatist, prose-writer, poet and folklorist. In his lyrics he tried to bring out the ancient features of Chuvash poetry, connected with the poetry of the Orient. Many of his poems have become popular songs.

Flax

Flax with your tresses
Of blue and green,
In your level sea
Sway and be glad.

Let the sun dance
Above you gaily,
And maiden's hearts
Caress and warm you.

Flax so shapely
With silken waist,
In your joy you cannot
See autumn's coming.

The lyre-hearted oriole
Will be soaked and grow sad,
And imperceptibly
Your flowers will yellow.

A girl will gather you
Stalk after stalk,
Bind you in sheaves
And dip you in the pond.

166

Water like a mother
Will embrace and caress you,
And there you will rest
In the pond's soft lap.

So your time will pass –
You will come to the beater,
The silvery combings
Be winnowed away.

A pestle of maple
Will dance all over you,
Not sparing a stitch
Of your fine clothing.

My old mother
Will light the stove
And lovingly comb
Your golden hair.

My sisters will spin you
By day and by night,
Making precious cloth
Of your golden fibres.

My older sister
Will sew me a white shirt,
Front and hem embroidered
With green and white.

Proudly and joyfully
I'll put on that shirt.
My dear brother-in-law
Will call me to the feast.

There for my songs
The women will love me
And offer me gifts
Of their fine embroidery.

And there I shall sing
A song in your honour
Flax with blue and green tresses
Swaying before me!

(1928)

167

Peter Khusankay

(Peder Khuzangay)

(1907–1970)

Born in the village of Sikterme in the Elkel district of Tataria, in the family of a poor peasant. Studied at the Kazan Pedagogical Institute of Eastern Peoples. His first book of poems appeared in 1928; his early work shows the influence of Yesenin and Mayakovsky. In the early 1930s he was the roving correspondent of the central Chuvash newspaper *Communard*, which was published in Moscow. In 1937 he was arrested on a charge of 'nationalism', spent a year in jail and was then acquitted. He fought in the Second World War and was seriously wounded. In 1950 he was awarded the honorary title of Chuvash People's Poet.

Khuazangay is one of the most important Chuvash poets, and has left a large body of work: a novel in verse, long poems, ten books of lyric poetry and articles about literature. He did excellent translations into Chuvash of many Russian and foreign classics, and also translated into Russian all the works of Kestenttin Ivanov and Mikhail Sespel. His own poems have been translated into Russian, and he has been published in Bulgarian, Georgian and Tatar.

The waters have not all drained

The waters have not all drained from the melted snows,
And the icy cold needles of the winds of spring
Pierce the earth's body, that is as crumbly as *khalva* . . .
Oh, how am I to make you feel all this?

On a summer night, bending away from the wind and
    toward it,
The heads of oats, already beginning to swell,
Like a soft pipe tune up their lament: *tyu-tyu-tyu* . . .
Oh, how am I to make you hear all this?

Early in the morning on the hushed, cool pond,
Now one, now another, in turn the grieving voices
Of autumn geese tremble in the air, then fall silent . . .
Oh, how am I to make you sympathise with this?

In winter the frosted eyelashes of the horse,
His familiar snorting as he treads his long road,
Remind us that all living souls are like our souls . . .
Oh, how am I to stop you forgetting this?

(1926)

(*khalva* – sweetmeat made of nuts, sugar and oil)

Songs of Tilli

(extracts)

I. *Farewell to the village on going off to be a soldier*

I bowed before the gates,
I drank from the cup of Welcome.

I bowed to the wide courtyard,
I drank from the cup of Concord.

I bowed down to the doorway,
I drank from the cup of Assurance.

I went into the house and bowed,
I drank from the cup of Fate.

I bowed to the people on the plank-beds,
I drank from the cup of Love.

I bowed and I said a poem,
I drank from the cup of Togetherness.

I bowed to the table in the corner,
I drank from the cup of Reverence.

I bowed, having sung a song,
I drank from the cup of Song for our Forefathers.

I bowed, having danced,
I drank from the cup of Completeness.

I waved my handkerchief, bowed to everyone,
And only then drank from the cup of the Road.

II. *What does the cock say to you?*

Scorching the lamp, the ember is fading,
Put no more birchwood spills in the holder:
The pane of your windows is growing blue;
The voice of the autumn cock rings out clearly.

170

Old men at your feasting table, listen –
What does the cock say to you?
'Instead of one day comes another', he says,
'It is not a day passing, but human life'.

Women, sitting together in your chamber,
What does the cock say to you?
'The woman with life is already dressing,
And you have still not got undressed'.

Dashing young men who go out of an evening,
What does the cock say to you? Listen:
'Dawn is breaking, it is time you went home,
You must not bring shame on your beloved'.

You beautiful girls, here's health to you!
And what is the cock saying to you?
'Burenka wants her drink in the cowshed,
It's time to be out there with your pails'.

Bright cheery children sleeping on benches,
Can you hear the merry cock-a-doodle doo?
'Auntie will soon be cooking pancakes,
Get up and eat them scorching hot'. . .

III. *My hair, my eyes*

A copper comb with a horse's head,
I always wore it on my belt.
I combed my head when I got up,
I combed my head when I went to bed –
And friend of my age, I didn't notice:
My hair was like a load of unmilled peas,
And now my head is bald as a threshing floor.

There were two broods of white chicks –
The two and thirty teeth in my head.
I picked up a corn-box with my teeth,
I bit through new hobbles of tough hemp –
And friend of my age, I didn't notice
How they all got loose, my broods,
And my white chickens all flew away.

171

My eyes were too strong for the hypnotist,
No doctor could look me in the eye.
I stared and my stare made the tree dry up,
I could tell my horse from two miles away,
Even by day I could see the stars –
When I die, alas, it will all be wasted,
For my eyes still see through everything,
To whom then can I bequeath my eyes?

(1933–40)

Salambi

to my daughter

I

Little one of mine!
How sad you're not older.
If you were, I would write you
Letters a yard long.

And how you could ever
Forget the soldier?
He remembers you tenderly,
Your man of sorrows.

His dug-out is only
A home when you are in it.
So give me your kisses! . . .
Death can't come near us.

II

Perching at the trench's mouth,
Swallows are twitter-twittering.
I had no time to take you out
In spring-time when the swallows sing,
For you to learn their pretty tongue.
Fare you well, my little one!

Bees go foraging about
For the snowdrops' golden mead.
I had no time to touch your mouth
With honeyed hand to make it sweet
In speaking – as I should have done.
Fare you well, my little one!

III

Day and night, the rain, the rain,
Leaden rain overhead . . .
Thank God at least you are close by,

Thank God you are far away.

Sometimes when all my strength has gone,
I look at your photograph –
And then I find my voice again . . .
And I try not to grow old.

Sometimes, even on the march,
I suddenly see fair hair
I see it stained with clotted blood –
And shuddering, I stop dead . . .

Day and night, the rain, the rain,
Leaden rain overhead . . .
Thank God at least you are close by,
Thank God you are far away.

(1942)

Mitta Vasleye

(Vasley Mitta)

(1908–1957)

By general consent Vasley Mitta is with Khuzangay the most important Chuvash poet since Sespel. He was born in the village of Asla Arabus in the Batyryal district. After attending the Ulyanovsk Pedagogical School, he worked as a teacher of his native language and a member of the radio committee. In 1937 he was arrested on a charge of 'nationalism' and spent seventeen years in prisons and labour camps. He died in his native village during the spring festival 'Agadui' with the words: 'The poet who dies on his native soil is happy'.

He did not leave a large volume of work; his lyric poetry only makes up one slim volume. But everything he wrote (including articles, sketches and diaries) is remarkable for its deeply felt inspiration, its thoughtfulness and its perfection.

Song of the land surveyor
(from the long poem 'Tair')

Measuring the land, I have walked fields and valleys
And in my thoughts I have found this song:

Blessed is our country, brother!
Always – in field after field – comes wheat.

The wheatfields do not lead us astray,
We are led astray by others' treasures.

The treasures of the world – tears of the oppressed –
Do not pine for them, for they bring disaster.

I have walked through many a field and valley;
I have made this song, and not without reason.

(end of the 1940s)

Song of the Lower Chuvash

Our wealth is little, no hoard of gold pieces,
We do not need much when our kinsfolk are with us.

Wealth is soon spent, and a little suffices,
But what is like living in harmony?

What we have is for all, what we lack is shared,
How, brothers, could it be otherwise?

Manna drops from heaven only very rarely,
But the wealth that is ours never dries up.

Best of the *Yr*, Thrift and Moderation,
You are our Happiness, Hope and Protection.

Let the old share their wisdom and the young their strength,
Man, always live at one with your fellows.

To you, clean House, strong in cheerful work,
Be honour and blessing and all pure gifts!

Honour and blessing in ages to come
To the corn of the Chuvash, salted with sweat!

(beginning of the 1950s)

(*Yr* – Chuvash spirits of good)

176

Song of the exiles

Through the star we see the way,
Through our tears we see the day . . .
(from a folksong)

Here, my wing, you must stay. Do not weep.
Let us part like soldiers, bravely.
My star way is long and straight.
My daylight through tears shines clearly.

The North Wind's freezing embrace
And the frost will caress us nightly.
The guard's medal shining brightly,
Will not let us lose our way.

We give thanks. We have been new fathered
By the ice age of Sarmandey.
Shall we sing, shall we smile at parting?
Perhaps parting for ever, my wife . . .

(1949?)

(*Sarmandey* – a tsar from a folk tale. Here, Stalin)

Message to friends

Do not forget those exiled to the depths.
Each of them has encountered his own fate.
To all of you, salaam! Your distant friend
Keeps up his spirit for the longed-for day.

Some time – by chance perhaps – that day will come,
And I shall burn with the same fire again,
No less than young folk at the *agadui,*
Or a master of the wedding with his guests.

I shall return meekly and terribly,
When my land begins once more its weddings.
I have composed my songs of inspiration,
Not to disgrace the wedding of my homeland.

Yes, the master of the wedding will return,
At midnight or by day – do not forget . . .
To all of you, salaam! Your distant friend
Will take into his house the festival! . . .

(end of the 1940s)

Elegy

The road that awaits me is a road unending,
And many are the sights I am destined to see . . .
My love, what has happened, what has struck us down?
At a time when we thought to live unmolested,
Again we must part – this is what has struck us.

You have remained far back in the distance.
Mountains, dark forests and rivers in flood
Have filled up these distances between us.
Assailed with curses, the wandering wild beast,
Wherever he looks, has found no place of peace.

Look, in front of my eyes a wide river is flowing,
Cold damp crawls upwards across the low earth.
I ran down to look: could it be my Volga?
No, these waters' breath is cold and unfriendly,
The flooded Ob, the icy root of the North.

Today it seems more than èver cruel,
Its waters are black and threatening.
Could it not greet us with words of welcome?
Or could it be we are unwanted guests?
Does the Chaldon not recognize the Chuvash?

To whom can I tell the sorrow that is in me?
To whom can I call, while I still have a tongue?
Work cannot help me, and my voice will perish.
From west to east, there are no pine forests,
Only the tangled undergrowth of grief.

There will come a time, and you will forget me.
How can you, like a bird accursed
Endure the life that will be yours to live?
The childish hope that you once gave to me,
You will bury it in a white calico shroud.

And I, still with my head unbowed,
Will wander and wander on my Calvary,
Through thickets and through waters and through
        mountains . . .
How could I call you, love, to come with me?
My distant road is one of grief and torment.

(1950)   (*Chaldon* – Chuvash of Siberia)

179

Above the steep stony bank

Above the steep, stony bank stands a little hut,
Covered with snow-drifts to the chimney . . .
Shurappa, open the door, let me in quickly,
I have barely managed to get home today.

The cold that takes your feet from under you
Has been wearing us down from morning to night.
Neither work nor fire can make us warm,
And the clothes we have are not clothes at all . . .

Light the fire, Shurappa, hang up the pot . . .
I shall take off my coat and sit and warm myself . . .
If it goes on like this any longer,
Life in this world will not be worth the living.

Each day you wear yourself out, work to the limit,
Crawling on your belly for the sake of work.
This dishonour which leaves us nothing human.
How much longer shall we endure it, brother?

Burn up, fire. Numbed strength, be born again,
Little by little come back to life.
We have still much to live and to endure,
And little time to live . . .
Come what may, whatever happens,
Keep on going! . . .

(early 1950s)

Epitaph
(inscribed on Mitta's grave in Asla Arabus)

What if I win no honour, no renown!
Let just one song of my thousand songs survive me,
And my brothers sing that song with heartfelt kindness,
And peace will be about me in my tomb.

(1956)

180

Stikhvan Shavly

(Stikhvan Shavly)

(1910–1976)

Born in the village of Chulsirma in the Shundal district of the Samara region. In the famine of 1921, he moved with his parents to Kharkov, and after his mother's death was brought up in a children's home. He studied at the Workers' Faculty of Samara and the Kazan Pedagogical Institute, then worked on the staff of newspapers and journals and the committee for radio information.

Gradually freeing himself from the powerful influence of Mayakovsky (many of whose works he translated), he wrote lyrical and epic poems which are highly expressive and full of striking imagery. He was awarded the title of Chuvash People's Poet.

Poppy field

Kerguri sowed poppies in his field,
Poppies flowered on every side.
They flowered like embroidery on the broad field,
The poppies – *chashtar, chashtar, chashtarika!*

And today we don't want to go back home,
Let us wander about in the field of poppies.
The poppies are red as the sun in the east,
And the cornflower blue is the eastern sky.

The girls as they walk are like the old image:
They are as fair as poppies in bloom.
And the poppy heads are like painted vessels,
The poppies – *chashtar, chashtar, chashtarika!*

Shall we not break these vessels open?
The smell that is in them might make us drowsy.
Kerguri has begun to blow his *sarnay*:
That means the choral dance is beginning.

With swaying heads the girls go singing.
I have said they are as fair as poppies,
Poppies in the full flower of life,
The poppies – *chashtar, chashtar, chashtarika!*

Work, work, by work you shall eat

As an eight-year old boy I climbed on the horse,
Just eight paces on I was thrown to the ground,
With a shake of its head the wormwood wished me well,
And the tiny lark blessed me with its song:
'Work, work, by work you shall eat!'

As a boy of eleven I saddled the harrow-horse,
Got three smacks from my father for harrowing badly,
With two shakes of its head the swan wished me well,
And the tiny bird blessed me with its song:
'Work, work, by work you shall eat!'

After ploughing fields I began to plough verse,
And I heard good words from people and bad,
Ringing three times, the milepost greeted me,
And the little bird blessed me with its song:
'Work, work, by work you shall eat!'

My hair has grown white, like silken feather grass,
But the little lark, my brother, has not deserted me,
It sits on my old shoulders, my kindly bird,
And seven times over it sings its blessing:
'Work, work, by work you shall eat!'

He who follows the plough, let him leave a straight furrow,
He who wields the hammer, let him make a merry din,
He who flies in the cosmos, let him sing to the Universe,
Let our own kindly bird greet us all with its blessing:
'Work, work, by work you shall eat!'

(1972)

(The refrain in Chuvash is an imitation of the lark's song)

Yakku Ukhsay

(Yakov Ukhsay)

(1911—)

Born in the village of Slakpus in the Belebeyev district of Bashkiria, in a poor peasant family. His grandfather was a close relative of Kestenttin Ivanov. He studied at Moscow University, then worked on the staff of the newspaper *Communard* and in the Bashkir Scientific Research Institute, and taught Chuvash language and literature in secondary schools. In 1950 he was awarded the honorary title of Chuvash People's Poet, and in 1972 he won the RSFSR Gorky Prize for Literature.

Ukhsay is the author of three verse novels, two tragedies and a number of long poems and lyric collections. His poetry is full of unusual imagery connected with a 'peasant' view of the world.

On a clear still summer night

On a clear still summer night
I gaze up at the moon.

Like its mother, a white cloud
Would lay it on soft down.

But it wants to see the world,
It climbs into the clear sky.

So my mother when I was a child
Tried to lull me to sleep.

But I ran off into the street
To see life and sing songs.

Since then I've had a moon-like face –
Now grey, I am all moon.

(1955)

Month of the sickle moon

Still I can see the faded moon.
The cocks' dialogue is done.
My dream, sweet as sherbet, still
Was creeping, creeping round my head –
But farewell my goose-down pillow!

Now on the river's other bank
Girls set off singing for the field,
And from their pitchforks and scythes
The shadows fall and break apart
As they go leaping over hills.

On willow tops jackdaws and crows
Have woken and begun their din.
Last night they only just were able
To fly home from the fields of rye;
Their throats crammed with stolen corn.

From olden days the Chuvash people
Have named this month for the sickle moon.
As patiently they toiled and sweated
Over their strips of ripening corn,
They glorified the fine-toothed sickle.

In heat like a burning stove
Do we not know how to wield a sickle?
And in that heat when we were babies
Did we not cry in our wicker cradles,
Our cradles rocking in the wind?

And in the blue eyes of the child
The world reflected was still brighter.
In the wind an owl flew past,
A cloud sailed over from the north,
The oak wood rocked and murmured.

The rye bread was my food then,
I got no cake from the bazaar,
Soup with dumplings was a feast.
I got the gift of writing poems
From the meat of the autumn lamb.

I am made of the riches of the field,
My body is hard as a rolling pin.
When I go to visit you
I always have to bow my head –
The door my father made is too small.

I have taken the Simbirsk reins
And drive the horses so vigorously
It makes them writhe like black snakes.
This speed comes to them from the meadow,
From the richness of the fields.

The sickle month has such abundance
It seems we shall never gather it all.
The cows' udders hang to the ground,
Each anthill is a treasure house,
In forest stumps the bees make riches.

The hamster has gathered in his lair
Lime seeds and yellow cobnuts.
And the corncrake – *pet-peltek* –
Can hardly lift up his full crop
And flies as heavily as lead.

Hotter and hotter grows the day.
The cornfield is as yellow as brass.
Argumentative and inspired,
The machines fill the air with noise –
Where is your sickle now, old month?

At night on the heavy boughs
The oriole sings more joyfully.
So as they look upon the wealth
Of autumn, let all men be happy
To hear my cheerful song!

(1935)

185

The bazaar of Ufim

I

When the red-hot coal of the sun had dropped
Gleaming through thin clouds on to the mountains,
The place I love, the bazaar of Ufim,
Began to hum with the wealth of autumn,
Full carts came streaming in from the fields.

I remember from childhood the noise of the bazaar,
We loved the jostle of the market people,
We listened to the pride of some rich man
Ringing boastfully in the clang of a copper bell
That hung from a roughly painted shaft-bow.

We watched the horse thieves from Piktesh
Haggling, the palms of their hands spread wide –
When they marched in, the poor people trembled,
They gave way, and looked down with humble faces,
But a spark of anger burnt invisibly in them.

The nights were black as the fields after ploughing.
A fire burned in the field like a haystack.
Subdued, we sat round it in a circle
And the whistling chiefs of crime came by,
Conspicuous, proud as the ace of spades.

And our poor horses the thieves had stolen
Whinnied sadly in the bazaars.
The merchants twisted their caps as a sign.
The buyers inspected the horses' teeth,
But we knew well what fine teeth they were.

The rich pedlars from Orenburg raised a din,
And they shone in the middle of the bazaar.
How magnificently the sun's embers sparkle!
They would sell them too, if it could be done,
And not care if the world was plunged in night.

Haven't we often seen two plucky dogs
Chasing the yellow fox in autumn?

186

Just so the untiring dog eyes of merchants
Follow the yellow circles of coins –
May the earth swallow up those dogs!

May the mice gnaw and eat their pockets!
May burning coals eat their money bags!
Not for us silver and copper, but bast!
We sold *lapti*, and bought white scarves
And offered them to our black-eyed beauties.

II

When the red-hot coal of the sun had dropped
Gleaming through thin clouds on to the mountains,
The place I love, the bazaar of Ufim,
Began to hum with the wealth of autumn,
Full carts came streaming in from the fields.

And now there appear on the streets of Ufim
Light winged flocks of girls from the Shuradal.
And the sweetness of cherries from flowered aprons,
The freshness of dew and the air of the mountains,
All this is reflected in their faces.

And the thick eyebrows steeply arched
Are like arches dipped in paint from Bugulma.
I would give them light-grey flaxen cloths
For my name among all the other names
To be embroidered there for ever.

Like a spark I gallop between the carts,
In my heart I give praise to the silver gleam
In the hands of my brother *kolkhoz* farmers;
Like a wedding master I pour out verses
Of praise to Kara-Akhmet the gardener.

Salaam-alec, old man, I know
That in the juice of your piles of melons
Is the wide night with its huge yellow moon,
And the sun itself, foaming with sparks,
And broad spaces and summers and springs.

My knife has a handle of bullock bone.
Let us cut a melon. Cross-legged I shall sit
And the dense meadow will rustle between us –
The nightingale whiteness of the bird cherry
Will be a circle around our feast.

Akhmet my friend, I have always loved you;
Your eyes are like cups of magic water.
I have watched the clouds floating by in them
And often with you, at the edge of the Urals,
I have drunk a cup of thick buttermilk.

On what horses have we not galloped together,
Unforgettable friend, on the grassy steppe!
I remember your hunting eagle, sitting
On your shoulder unmoving as you galloped,
With wings stretched two yards wide.

Having grown up in strength like that eagle,
In my journey through life I never tire,
Noisy as the poplar on the banks of Huradal,
My speech is in songs, like the wedding master,
Joyful and clear like the waters of Shuradal.

Through the cherry's whiteness, over *kolkhoz* melons,
We gaze at each other now, my friend.
We no longer remember our family quarrels,
Lightly we part and go out to the fields,
Whistling gaily between our teeth.

Where once walked the horse thieves, now long forgotten,
I cheerfully walk through the dense rejoicing
And hear the oriole fluting in its cage,
On the stalls the heavy, golden-combed cocks
Are crowing lustily here and there.

Resound day and night, bazaar of Ufim!
Display our treasures, shine in their plenty!
How happy our age! Let this be your music.
Let our shoulders be covered with shining fur,
And our seat be on the carpet of honour!

(1939)

Aleksey Vorobyov

(Aleksey Vorobyov)

(1922–1976)

Born in the village of Man Yaush in the Vurnar district. Attended agricultural college and worked as an agronomist. In 1942 he was seriously wounded at Stalingrad. On returning to his native village, he was chairman of the collective farm and director of the machine tractor station. After 1957, he made his living as a writer. He was awarded the Mikhail Sespel prize for Chuvash literature.

Cocks

There are twelve towels in the young girl's chest,
Each of them was twelve days embroidering.
The patterns are of cocks, cock after cock . . .
Their wings just lifted, ready to fly.

In the yard at midnight a crowing of cocks –
No, the girl will never get off to sleep.

Of whom is she thinking that she cannot rest?
If she should but sleep, it's the same in her dreams:
Cocks' wings flapping and cocks shouting –
Trying to escape from the chest to freedom.

Where is the man for whom all this is done?
Without him the chest will remain unopened.

(1963)

Autumn shone forth

Autumn shone forth . . . Then grew dark.
But the world still has life-giving colour:
In the withered flower's dry eye
A new seed gleams like a spark.
So small . . . But the spring will come,
And this seed will be strong enough
To illuminate this drab
And empty place with its light.

(1967)

Nikolay Sandrov

(Nikolay Sandrov)

(1922 —)

Born in the village of Chyuksirmi in the Tovay district. After serving in the war, he attended the Chuvash Pedagogical Institute and worked in the State Publishing House. He is one of the best educated of Chuvash poets, and often deals with modern city life and the problems of the modern intelligentsia.

Our people do not say

Our people do not say: 'Women are washing the floor,'
But say: 'Our daughter-in-law is *lighting* the floor' . . .
And indeed it is *lit* so brightly
That no speck of dust trips the sun.

When after some weary journey
You enter a house so clean
At first you dare tread nowhere –
Everything gleams with soap.

But then you sit there and look
At the floor white as homemade cheese,
You rest in whiteness and light
In your childhood, a feeling of home.

(1965)

Valentin Urtash

(Valentin Urdash)

(1924–1973)

Urdash may be called the 'minstrel' of Chuvash poetry. From 1946, when he became a professional writer, he had no permanent residence, but travelled through Chuvashia and much of Tataria, reading poems and singing songs. Many of his poems have become popular songs.

He was born in the village of Rakkassi in the Buva district of Tataria. On finishing secondary school in 1943, he went to the front and was seriously wounded, losing one eye and his right arm, and being crippled in his left arm. After a long stay in hospital, he returned home as an invalid. Now his name is one of the most honoured in Chuvash literature.

In war too

In war too I have this dream:
Mother is drying *shirttan*.
Father loses his cap at a feast
And has to walk home bare-headed.

They say drying *shirttan* is unlucky . . .
I don't think it's unlucky, this dream.
For three months I've not written, sister,
Letters can't pass the enemy lines.

They say losing a cap is unlucky,
But my dream's not unlucky, believe me.
I'm alive, but cut off, and my letters
Can't reach you, sister, but write.

You know who I'd like to hear from.
Tell her all my wishes, sister.
Now she will be cutting rye . . .
Nothing but snakes in the field.

Yes, in war too you dream dreams.
You see friends and enemies.
What if I dreamed of a lost cap –
Appa, I shall be back.

(1942)
(*shirttan* – a kind of Chuvash sausage; *appa* – sister)

Wounded

Do not tell my father of wounds,
They will be like wounds to him too.

Take care of him, only let him see me
When I am a man again, sister.

I will be a man again, believe me,
I shall walk our street as before.

'A real soldier', my father will say,
He won't weep because I am crippled.

Don't tell mother I have lost an eye,
Let her not weep for that.

Take care of her, only let her see me
When I am a man again, sister.

Does she dream of a good daughter-in-law?
She will see me walking the street with her.

Do not tell my love I have lost my arms,
Lost my arms and lost one eye.

I have no arms, no eye, no looks,
But I shall come home and live.

I am wounded, scorched for my brothers,
Let them speak kindly of me, sister.

(1943)

193

A leksey A fanasyev

(Aleksey Afanasyev)

(1925 —)

Born in the village of Potapovo-Tumbaria in the Bavla region of Tataria.
Educated in the Udmurt collective farm school and worked as a teacher of
Udmurt language and literature. Fought in the Second World War, and after
the war worked as a village school teacher and edited a local newspaper. He
is a poet, a prose writer and a dramatist, and has translated Ivanov's *Narspi*
and other works of Chuvash literature into Udmurt.

Suddenly in the stove

Suddenly in the stove a spark shoots out in the air –
It is an omen that guests are on their way.
Our plank bed is covered with an embroidered rug,
The cat sits washing its ear with its paw.
The ancient gate to the street sings in the wind,
And the gate post survives from a century ago.
What cold, wet people have come in through the gate! . . .
How many guests have gone out singing through it! . . .

Perhaps it is their song that the gate still hums,
Peering out at the road and the drifting snow? . . .

(1964)

Gratitude

I

My forest, I tried to take notice
Of your kindness to me as a boy.
The dreaming wind murmured through you,
The sun's red ball hid within you.

You never closed your door on me;
In your deep, fresh-seeming darkness
How often my heart shone silently
With thanks to you, the unspeaking!

II

My field, how freely the wind
Roams through you with soft light mane!
Oh, to saddle this unseen horse,
To take hold of its silken reins!

The rainbow would be my shaft-bow,
The lark would ring like a sleigh-bell,
I should lose myself in your waves,
Rippling in green, blue and gold.

III

My hills with your gold-green head-dress,
Your grass is like old men's hair.
But my eyes have never seen
Deep antiquity like yours.

You sleep, now and then you sigh,
And old scars of fire and sea
Open up on your lions' heads,
When the wind and my love caress you.

(1964)

Georgy Efimov

(Georgy Efimov)

(1928—)

Born in the village of Malti Antavash in the Kanash district. Studied in the drama school of the Chuvash State Theatre and the Gorky Literary Institute in Moscow. For many years director of the literary review *Yalav*. His poetry shows the successful combination of modern themes with the ancient moral traditions of the Chuvash.

Words spoken at the beginning of the sowing by the one who throws the first handful of seed

Oh, sunny-golden grain,
The sun looks down on you,
The wind blows from one side,
As if to stir you to act!
Below the earth awaits you,
Spreading and lifting up
Its friendly warmth for you.
So stir yourself in the earth,
Do not slumber and yawn,
Peck moisture like a bird,
Shake yourself and tremble,
Shake and throw off the earth,
Come forth as a bold shoot!
Reach up towards the sun,
Take on yourself its likeness,
Be the image of the sun!
Reach higher still and higher
And pull us after you;
And afterwards be the ground
And basis of our life,
Become the firm foundation
Of all our hopes and dreams;
You are our joy and grief;

Igniting joy within us,
Shine forth in your own light,
Grow into a cornfield
Like a wood of young oaks –
Shine in unending breadth
With joy and inspiration,
With happiness and strength!

197

Gennady Aygi

(Gennady Aygi)

(1934—)

The compiler of the present anthology, born in the village of Shaymurzino in the southern part of the Chuvash Republic. His father, who was killed in World War II, was a teacher of Russian, and his mother came from a line of pagan priests. He studied at the Gorky Literary Institute, and has lived mainly in Moscow over the past thirty years. His early poems were written in Chuvash, and he continues to work in his native tongue, but is principally known as one of the most important poets currently writing in Russian. For further details, see the biographical note on page i.

Let me be in your midst

let me be in your midst
a dusty coin turning up
among rustling banknotes
in a slippery silk purse:
it would ring at the top of its voice
but there's nothing hard to ring on

when double-basses boom
and memory tells
how in childhood the wind
smoked with rain on autumn mornings

let me be
a standing coatrack
on which you can hang
not raincoats only
but something besides
that weighs more than a coat
and when I stop believing in myself
let memory of veins
make me firm again
and again I shall feel
the eye muscles' pressure

(1954)

Snow

From the nearby snow
the flowers on the sill are strange.

Smile to me if only because
I do not speak the words
that I shall never understand.
All that I can say to you is this:

chair, snow, eyelashes, lamp.

And my hands
are simple and distant,

and the window frames
seem cut from white paper,

but there, beyond them,
around the lamp-post,
whirls the snow
from our very childhood.

And will go on whirling while people
remember you on earth and speak with you.

And those white flakes I once
saw in reality,
and I shut my eyes and cannot open them,
and the white sparks whirl,

and I am not able
to stop them.

(1959)

Vasily Endip

(Vasily Endip)

(1937—)

Born in the village of Khura Shyv in the Kuybyshev region. Worked as a
railwayman and an electric welder. Took a degree by correspondence at the
Chuvash State University and worked in a publishing house. Today he is a
professional writer. In contemporary Chuvash poetry, where the epic strain
has become rare, Endip is one of the few writers who has been successful
with longer narrative poems.

Lark

With a tremble and flutter of wings, singing in inspiration,
    The lark is climbing skywards –
    Higher he climbs, still higher.
Hangs there on a level and sings: Ah, earth is down there,
                        down there!
    But the sky keeps on calling, calling –
    And the flyer's fear is vanquished.
And he beats his wings and flies, climbing still higher and
                        higher.
    How good he feels as he flies
    And measures the boundless sky!
The bird looks up to the heights and sees the inviting sun.
    He looks down below, to the earth –
    And something clutches his heart . . .
But he does not cease to glory in his own intrepid flight! –
    He sings while he still has breath,
    He flies, till he slips and slides,
And plummets to earth's embrace, where he takes a
                        moment's rest,
    And then up again to the heights,
    And from the sky back to earth, then sky –
A hundred, a thousand times over – spring to autumn,
                        morning to night . . .

    Is it happiness, is it pain?
Human soul, there is your fate.

(1977)

Yury Aydash

(Yury Aydash)

(1938—)

Aydash, a master craftsman, has written outstanding philosophical lyrics, and has translated Hungarian and Polish poetry. He was born in the village of Syavalkassi in the Burnar district, attended the Kazan State University, and now works in a publishing house. He has been awarded the Mikhail Sespel prize.

Girls going visiting, 1945

Slowly night draws the curtain,
Shyly the first star gleams.
Day's bustle is subsiding,
But earth still holds its warmth.

Dark looms the willow thicket,
Dogs are barking now and then . . .
Sleepy and tired, the village
Draws a deep, weary breath.

But look . . . shining white ahead there,
Headscarves one after another . . .
A balalaika calls to the dance.
Silently girls are weeping.

(1971)

There is a time

There is a time like this –
Tired and indifferent
A gentle drizzle drips . . .
The bed is still not made.

As if the busy world
Had slightly turned your head,
You do not feel time pass,
Forgetting all your cares.

You look out on the yard
With glazed and misty eyes,
Speaking of something vague
With silent rain-soaked leaves.

Your wife and child are there –
Softly they call your name.
With a remorseful voice,
'Yes, mother, yes', you say.

(1972)

Gennady Yumart

(Gennady Yumart)

(1938—)

'Yumart is the poet of those subtle and rare feelings of harmony between the inner world and the outer', writes the literary scholar Atner Khuzangay, noting that he is skilful in 'giving an archaic tone to poetic language', especially in works where he recalls the ancient ethical foundations of the Chuvash view of the world. He was born in the village of Kayri Karok in the Krasnoarmeysky district, attended the Chuvash State Pedagogical Institute and has a senior position in the Chuvash Research Institute.

Flower of heaven
(for the painting 'White Flower' by V. Yakovlev)

If the mass of disaster crushes my head,
If sorrowful days oppress and surround me,

I take refuge, I come and I stand before you,
My lost soul receives your gift of patience.

All sufferings, all the sorrow of earth,
You have taken upon yourself alone –

And as a high emblem of holiness,
You shine, shine whitely in love's radiance.

(1970)

(Vladimir Yakovlev, born 1934, is an outstanding representative of the contemporary avant-garde in Russian art.)

Rook snowstorm

Whether for luck or what,
But such is her way,
Suddenly winter, departing,
Swirls her treasure of snows.

You walk through the white world,
White snow blinds the eyes.
You see and hear only snow,
Only snow you feel.

So the rooks from far away
Have flown with news of the spring,
And secretly they wait,
Hiding behind this snowstorm.

It seems as if any time,
Nearby, somewhere they will answer.
It seems that the branches already
Long to see them again.

Winter, we see, is politely
Taking her leave of us,
Showering us with the honour
Of her final snowflakes.

In our honour the rook snowstorm
Heaps her treasures on us,
As if saying: 'Look, remember
My snows' white innocence'.

Mikhail Seniel

(Mikhail Seniel)

(1940—)

The range of 'poetic variations' of this poet is quite considerable – from romanticism in the style of Grin (the pseudonym Seniel is the name of a hero of the Russian romantic writer A.S. Grin) to a vigorous expressionism, which is particularly interesting in that it shows itself in the bold, innovative treatment of motifs from Chuvash folklore. He was born in the village of 'Urmandeyevo in the Aksubay district of Tataria. After attending Kazan State University, he worked in a publishing house, but now lives by his writing.

Your blessing!

Now is the time to start, my road will be long.
I do not ask for wealth – I am my own riches.
I'm rich – an arse, a head, a pair of hands –
How's that for capital, for working assets?

Your blessing, mother, let me have your blessing,
Your blessing, father, let me have your blessing!

My two long legs are like two striding poles.
Away from home they're bound to come in handy.
Just what I'll need to go running after someone
Or to run away if they come after me.

Your blessing, mother, let me have your blessing,
Your blessing, father, let me have your blessing!

The body's there to wave its arms about,
And arms to clench their hands up into fists,
A head not to be taken from the shoulders
To satisfy the whim of some fine scoundrel.

Your blessing, mother, let me have your blessing,
Your blessing, father, let me have your blessing!

I'll never grovel, my head will never let me,
Won't hang my head, my soul will not allow it.
When there's nothing left, I still possess a soul,
And isn't that wealth enough, for Heaven's sake!

Your blessing, mother, let me have your blessing,
Your blessing, father, let me have your blessing!

Yury Semender

(Yury Semender)

(1941 —)

A poet with a 'peasant' vision, a 'husbandman' approach to the surrounding world. He was born in the village of Tanosh in the Krasnoarmeysky district, attended the Chuvash State University, and is the editor-in-chief of the journal *Yalav*.

Foal

All shining in the light of day
with bright sides, thin legs,
the month-old foal is a coin
fresh-minted by the sun.

With his mother, day after day,
he ambles off to work –
caught by some sight, lags behind,
then races to catch up.

He walks by her side, as if taking
some of her load himself,
the mother feels this presence
and pulls more easily.

Snowdrifts in spring

The spring sun
melts like butter,
but down below
the snowdrifts are undefeated:
with bristles erect,
they still stare fiercely,
like stubborn wild boars
refusing to die.

207

Aleksey Attil

(Aleksey Attil)

(1943–1979)

The leading post-war Chuvash poet. In his early writing he was influenced by the Chuvash poetry of Gennady Aygi and the Russian poetry of Boris Pasternak (which he translated into Chuvash). In the high tragic tone of his mature work he resembles Sespel. For further details, see the Epilogue, pp. 218–9.

When it has happened

And somewhere
in the hushed wood
(no trace, no path)
is something:
is it a store
or a cabin . . .
I only know: it has boards for windows.
This place is guarded by the hornet.
It is his
dark work.

There, perhaps,
the seconds drip,
secretly threatening.
And there you wake.
As if carrying you somewhere,
the hornet
drones.
He sets out – with buzzing designs – all you have known
(somewhere too – your childhood games)
and as he flies, he snaps
at once
your memory.

Peder Eyzin

(Peder Eyzin)

(1943—)

Eyzin, along with Attil (his close friend) is the most important of the post-Thaw generation of Chuvash poets. He had a great influence on the poets of the 70s and 80s (for further details, see the Epilogue, p. 220–2). He was born in the village of Enekhmetin in the Elek district, attended the Chuvash State Pedagogical Institute, and for over twenty years has been working for the Chuvash State Publishing House.

Waterdrop

A drop,
the first to feel the spring,
detaches itself
and loudly
falls;
and, plunged in thought a moment,
the world
listens.

No-one has yet
awakened.

And again
the drip.
And again
the listening world.

The star looks

The star looks,
the star sees –
in this world
lives a simpleton.

The moon looks,
the moon sees –
in this world
lives a simpleton.

The sun looks,
The sun sees –
in this world
lives a simpleton.

No mind at all,
no strength at all,
and still he lives,
that simpleton.

No colour in his face,
no clothes to wear,
and still he lives,
that simpleton.

No good name at all,
no honour at all,
and still he lives,
that simpleton.

The star sees –
the moon sees –
the sun sees –
who is he then?

He is me, that simpleton.

Peder Yakkuzen

(Peder Yakkuzen)

(1950—)

A quiet, thoughtful poet, whom one might perhaps describe as the wisest of his generation. He was born in the village of Ubasirmi in the Krasnoarmeysky district, and is a university teacher of Chuvash literature.

In the September light

In the September light
The fields of Chuvashia
Are tidy, modest, sad,
Like an empty house
When the children are gone,
Long since grown up.
September light! The soul's world
Is filled with sorrow,
When the sound of snapped straw
Resounds in deserted space,
Heralding rain.
Yes, soon they will come,
The rains, one after another,
But we shall live through them
As if in hiding
In the September light,
still shining in memory,
as quiet as ever,
as modest and pure.

Epilogue:
Recent Developments in
Chuvash Poetry

For the reasons given in the Introduction, I originally limited this anthology to writers born before 1930. The poets born since then, and particularly those who began writing in the years 1960–1980, are very numerous – 'every shepherd with us is a poet, every tenth Chuvash writes poetry', said Peder Khuzangay. Naturally, it is hard to say at present which of them will leave a lasting mark in our literature.

In any case, the 'generation of the 1960s to the 1980s' is very active, and its poetry shows remarkable breadth and intensity. One might even speak of a second Renaissance in Chuvash culture after its stormy neap-tide of the 1920s. In comparison with that time, the poets of the present generation (who are more numerous because of improved educational opportunities and better material conditions) are much freer in the search for a personal world view and in their creative experiments.

One could say that until the present time the European influence on Chuvash literature was vague and ill-defined; one could detect only distant echoes, coming by way of Russian literature. The younger generation now has the opportunity of more direct access to the major products of European culture, particularly important being their acquaintance with French Impressionism, and with certain aspects of contemporary European philosophy. There has been an upsurge of activity on the part of the Chuvash intelligentsia, whose linguistic and literary horizons are no longer confined to their native language. Young poets are beginning to show a lively interest in the poetry of various countries, such as France, Poland, Hungary and the Latin-American countries, by way of translations into Russian and Chuvash.

In what follows I want to indicate briefly the tendencies

213

that seem to me to define the present state of Chuvash poetry. These are most clearly visible in the generation of the sixties to the eighties, so I shall base what I have to say on these relatively recent publications, both in book form and in the periodical press.

In one way or another, the poets in question are striving to transcend national limits. It has to be said, however, that the 'grey mass' of contemporary Chuvash poetic production resembles the same sort of grey mass in run-of-the-mill Russian poetry; it is as if our mediocre national poets were translating this verse into their own clichéd language. But in this mass of verse one can distinguish three interwoven threads of living development in contemporary Chuvash poetry.

The first may be called the *Sespel-European* line. This tendency has always been the channel for Russian and European influence in Chuvash poetry, attempting to overcome national limitations and to express itself with maximum intensity in a Westernizing manner. In the literature of small nations, poetry of this European type calls for particular individuality on the part of the poet, much more so than the 'national' (and in many respects 'folkloric') tendency. 'Latent in language is a philosophical mythology', wrote Nietzsche; in the culture of small nations, which have over the centuries established for themselves an identity relatively uninfluenced by Western Europe, the entire poetic language becomes a kind of concealed mythology, and only a small number of exceptional individuals are able to break out of these confines. Moreover, this break leads to personal tragedy, and the very shape and texture of the 'new word' is marked by dislocation.

In Chuvash poetry, it was Mikhail Sespel who first made this tragic breakthrough. In the 1960s, characteristics reminiscent of Sespel showed themselves in the figure of Aleksey Attil (1943–1979), the most striking contemporary Chuvash poet writing in the 'European' manner. His dramatic attempts to break out of the 'popular-mythological' confines bear the scars of deeply national consciousness, and this gives his work a dualistic character – at the same time national and homely and unconsciously existentialist – which is unusual among the Chuvash.

The influence of Boris Pasternak is perceptible in Attil's early poems, for instance 'March':

214

March.
Air clean as a lens.
In the light of the moon,
in the frost,
snowdrifts breathe silently –
as if frost soothed their torment.

The dirty distance shining with waters
is magic not only with expectation:
there is a healthy, penetrating purity
in March's disorder.

The following short poem, written at the end of the 1960s, is more typical of Attil:

Bird cherry and apple.
Beehives.
The oak woods fence is mouldy
with tiny fungi.
And the sky, on the point of collapsing
on the palisade.
Oh, no!

Heaven does not recognize us.
This is my one and only
love that I did not save –
down, straight down
on the spikes of the fence!

Attil, like Sespel, had a short literary career. He worked as a village schoolteacher, and in 1969 fell victim to severe mental illness. He lived for ten years alone in his village with his old mother, writing almost no poetry, and died in a psychiatric hospital in Kazan. His death, which was a great loss to Chuvash culture, went almost unnoticed.

In the last twenty years, the Sespel tradition has increasingly absorbed the stream of Chuvash lyric poetry which can be called *popular-philosophical* and is connected with the clear, wise poetry of Vasley Mitta. In a recent book by Nikolay Ismukov (born in 1942), I came across not only poems in the Mitta tradition, but purely philosophical poems such as the following:

215

> *On this hill,*
> *Like the commander of some army,*
> *I control with my eyes*
> *The flashing movement of all about me.*
>
> *Is it truth in it or deception*
> *That creates this impenetrability?*
> *Hooped in, I cannot escape*
> *From this circle of Beauty.*
>
> *No, not the commander of an army,*
> *But a captive, encircled by this miracle.*
> *Nowhere can I take this treasure that surrounds me,*
> *Nor can I possess and master it here.*

The second tendency which is most active in contemporary Chuvash lyric may be described as *national and formally innovative*. It is as if the young poets had begun to recall vividly the fundamental ethical and aesthetic principles of their people and to reconstruct them in new poetic forms. Whether these are 'recitatives' or modernized 'songs', they all have one thing in common: they are written in free verse. Originally a variant of European *vers libre* (firstly in the work of Sespel, and then in my own early poems of the 1950s), this kind of poetry spread quickly and took on a specifically Chuvash character. The original European and modernist element in it fused in an unexpected manner with another element, the forgotten language of the ancient spells and incantations of the pagan Chuvash.

Beginning in the work of the remarkable poet Peder Eyzin (born in 1943), this was a largely unconscious process. Eyzin himself began as an innovator in the Sespel tradition. In the mid-sixties he was writing free verse, every poem being the working out of an everyday metaphor. Here, as an example, is the poem 'Dew':

> *'I am the nightingale's tear.*
> *I am silence.*
> *No-one*
> *Can hear me.*
>
> *I am less than a star.*

Nobody
Even notices me . . .'

Midnight.
With piercing eyes the drop of dew
Stared at the moon.

The European narrative and enumerative types of free verse
are not to be found in Eyzin's work, any more than the ellip-
tical and paradoxical types. In his free verse could be heard
for the first time echoes of the archaic forms of Chuvash folk
song – let me quote a 'song' of the 1960s:

We are fine fellows,
and you are fine fellows,
finer fellows than us
there are.

We are rich,
and you are rich,
richer folk than us
there are.

We are fools,
and you are fools,
bigger fools than us
there are not.

There followed a kind of 'rememoration' or poetic 'recon-
struction' of the unwritten foundations of the popular moral
code. Soon Eyzin's poems took on the character of 'circular
spaces' growing out of a core of popular sayings and proverbs,
or else they modelled themselves on the parallelism of
ancient Chuvash songs, but with a genuinely contemporary
appearance:

If you are not hungry,
do not take bread:
nothing is dearer
than bread.

> *If you have not washed your hands,*
> *do not take bread:*
> *nothing is cleaner*
> *than bread.*

> *If you have not taken off your cap,*
> *do not take bread,*
> *nothing is older*
> *than bread.*

The way in which Eyzin conveys the ancient artistic material which he has 'dug up' often reminds me, paradoxically (but quite properly, I think), of modernist poetic experiments in such varied literature as those of Turkey (for instance, the poems of Orhan Veli) or the Baltic countries. I remember how fifteen years ago Eyzin expressed genuinely Zen Buddhist ideas about poetry to me, though knowing nothing of Zen Buddhism. On another occasion he spontaneously exclaimed about 'ordinary' Chuvash poetry of today: 'What a lot of words they use! How I wish poetry could be a simple statement, like "A bird sat on a telegraph post and sang"!' And subsequently Eyzin did indeed write such poems:

> *A dark*
> *day.*
> *In autumn mud*
> *green*
> *winter corn.*

Towards the end of the 70s, many young poets seem to have thought that they had cracked Eyzin's code. This 'code' was immediately set to work, and now, under his influence, there is a considerable amount of free verse which resembles flat and utterly unpoetic moral exhortations. In fact, it has to be said that in general, free verse on the Eyzin model quickly became free verse of a *didactic, formulaic* type. He himself, in the search for something new, stopped publishing.

Free verse has by now become a normal feature of Chuvash poetry. There have been free-form poems written in the manner of ancient pagan prayers, 'charms' such as those found in the work of Lyubov Martyanova (born in 1950). Most of her 'meditations' are made up of contrasting or ever more powerful definitions of a single image throughout an entire poem – one stanza can serve as an example:

> *The boat sailed without an oar.*
> *Like a word unspoken,*
> *Like a faith abandoned,*
> *Like a shy smile.*

Young poets have begun to strive after more striking and unusual images. In the poems of another woman poet Raisa Sarbi (born 1951), we find comparisons such as this:

> *The sun*
> *sits on the saksaul branch*
> *with legs crossed*
> *like a Turkmen.*

Indeed, the achievements of contemporary European art are increasingly important for Chuvash authors. Thus a frequent concern of Porfiry Afanasyev-Akhavan (born 1942) in his short poems is the solving of 'spatial problems':

> *Ice melting on the Volga, melting ice,*
> *Something floats off down river, something stays,*
> *Something is accomplished, passes on,*
> *Something continues – like a vague desire.*
>
> *Here below, on the Volga, is the ice,*
> *And above it flames the song of the lark,*
> *And for me it is a riddle to be solved –*
> *That singing poised between the ice and the sun.*

In the context of Chuvash poetry, the work of Boris Chindykov (born 1960) has an almost avant-garde appearance. The alienated 'objectivity' of his poems is expressed in an unusual style of hard precision, 'anti-metaphorical' like that of his Polish and Baltic contemporaries:

> *having gained freedom*
> *in love without love*
> *having found myself and peace*
> *I am afraid to stop loving you – and so*

219

> *I love nothing except*
> *your pride*
> *nothing*

Let me conclude these remarks on the present state of Chuvash poetry with a brief mention of a third tendency, the *traditional-popular*, which is based on folklore. It can be said that nowadays the stylizing approach to this 'inexhaustible' spring is dying out. The poets of this third tendency, writing poems which are almost folkloric in form, attempt to find bolder ways of transforming images and metaphors taken from oral literature. Here for instance are some well-known words from a choral dancing song: 'The bird cherry in its flowering can be seen the whole forest through'. This image is twice transposed by the poet Veniamin Pegil (born 1955) in the following short piece:

> *Through the whole forest the white cherry can be seen,*
> *Through the whole forest it turns my head.*
> *Again I see myself young at seventeen*
> *In the very heart of the dancing ring.*
>
> *Through the whole forest the white cherry can be seen,*
> *Through the whole forest its whiteness flames.*
> *Do not touch, leave its whiteness in the forest,*
> *Leave my youth still youthful in the dancing ring.*

The various tendencies of modern Chuvash poetry which I have described all come together and interweave in the creative efforts of our young writers.

Gennady Aygi
Moscow, October 1983